Current Trends in Correctional Education: Theory and Practice

Current Trends in Correctional Education: Theory and Practice

Sol Chaneles, PhD
Editor

The Haworth Press
New York

Current Trends in Correctional Education: Theory and Practice has also been published as *Journal of Offender Counseling, Services & Rehabilitation,* Volume 7, Numbers 3/4, Spring/Summer 1983.

The Haworth Press, Inc., 10 Alice Street, Binghamton, NY 13904–1580

Library of Congress Cataloging in Publication Data
Main entry under title:

Current trends in correctional education.

"Current trends in correctional education : theory and practice has also been published as Journal of offender counseling, services & rehabilitation,
Volume 7, numbers 3/4, Spring/Summer 1983"—T.p. verso.
Includes bibliographical references.
1. Juvenile delinquents—Education—United States—Addresses, essays, lectures.
2. Prisoners—Education—United States—Addresses, essays, lectures.
I. Chaneles, Sol.
HV9081.C87 1983 365'.66 83-18542
ISBN 0-86656-268-0

Current Trends in Correctional Education: Theory and Practice

Journal of Offender Counseling, Services & Rehabilitation
Volume 7, Numbers 3/4

CONTENTS

Preface

Financing Prison Education in the United States

I stood at control gate number one in the world's largest prison. It was the occasion of my first visit to a place of involuntary incarceration. The main corridor was so long you could actually see, or sense, the earth's curvature. The island on which the prison stood had been made from "fill"—hundreds of millions of tons of garbage sloughed off by millions of neighbors across the bay living in the world's richest city. The number of prisoners there, plus the guards and civilian employees on an island slightly over six hundred acres in size gave the place a population density greater than the Bombay slums. It was at this complex and sullen place that I was struck with the reality and potential of prison education.

The prison's school, mandated by state law for young offenders of "mandatory" school age—fifteen to seventeen, consisted of three rooms improvised from narrow, abandoned warehouses that had once stored spare parts for missile-launching equipment. In the early 1950s, a missile launching site had been constructed on the tiny island so that if the distant enemy attacked the site, mainly the condemned and their custodians would be wasted. No certified or licensed school teacher sought employment at this school. In spite of such incentives as a three hour work day, twenty per cent more pay than other school teachers and classroom discipline maintained by guards in uniform, jobs were filled by the discouraged, the unfit and the rejected. Often, classes were canceled and the school shut down because teachers did not show up for work. School texts were rejects scheduled for shredding to pulp. The "school library" consisted of a single, collapsing three shelf bookcase with not over twenty non-descript book-like objects that had been donated by an anonymous benefactor. During that very period of time, the Superintendent of Schools of the richest city in the world, had his personal yacht outfitted with luxurious fittings and furnishings, fueled and maintained at public expense, all in secret, all illegal and all with the unpaid, mandatory labor of the involuntarily incarcerated boys of mandatory school age. During the same period of time, the prison's supervisor of rehabilitation, related by marriage to the prison's chief, received a secret salary supplement from funds officially earmarked for the education of the young prisoners.

It is difficult to erase from memory the blank, unused walls of the seemingly endless corridors. The hundreds of thousands of square feet of walls were unadorned by a single word, a single image, a single slogan on the majesty of Law, a single graffito.

Of prison education elsewhere I have been witness to these things.

The education room of a South Carolina prison in which forty prisoners are ordered to stand in silence for five hours, doing nothing because the materials with which they were to learn techniques of mending school books had not been delivered.

The automotive classroom of a major prison in Pennsylvania consisting of only half an automobile. The other half, cut from its other part by acetylene torch lay in the prison yard. The classroom had been placed on the prison's second floor in a room that could accommodate only half a car and no tools.

An entire education building of a major New York State prison shut down because the prison's entire education budget for one year had been secretly and improperly diverted by the prison's superintendent to repair his official car badly wrecked in an accident by his partying daughter.

The education program in the county juvenile jail of the nation's most highly industrialized state, within minutes of the sleek international headquarters of a multi-billion dollar multi-national corporation: a single, windowless room with no ventilation. Inside, a dozen, sleepy youngsters overseen by a corpulent retired school principal who smokes a cigar as he fondles juvenile genitalia. No books. No blackboards. No maps, white paste, stuffed animals or the amorphous incunabula of schoolrooms past and dimly remembered.

The entire vocational education program of the principal penitentiary of Minnesota: a single, ten foot by twelve foot space closed off from its surroundings by six foot high plywood panels located in the prison's sub-basement a few feet from the institution's generator whose noise level prohibits both conversation and teaching.

The word "disgrace" cannot adequately characterize the schools, school programs and education I have witnessed in prisons of Texas, Arizona, Mississippi, Ohio, and anywhere. In a Louisiana prison the sole classroom was used exclusively for providing inmates, ten at a time, with a chance (for fees and sexual favors) to become "high" by means of sniffing highly volatile "glue." In Florida, schoolrooms were converted into locker rooms for accountants and bookkeepers. In the nation's capital, for a very long time, prisons had no classrooms, education, or teachers.

A number of times, over the span of a generation, I have seen notable efforts to bring the much vaunted blessings of education to prisons through the creation of "education-school districts." Indeed, at one time, it appeared that these districts would catch on, take hold and work. They lasted a few years, were mandated out of existence and these few words are probably the only consecration of their memory. To date, the noble experiment in education-school districts for prisons has not caused a single scholarly article or dissertation.

A number of times, over the span of a generation, I have been called upon to testify at legislative committee meetings on the subject of education for prisoners. The word "disgrace" cannot adequately characterize the chaos, the barrenness, the shabby indifference.

With hardly any change over the span of a generation the following figures tell the tale:

— less than one half of one per cent of the total operating budget for all prisons in the nation is allocated to all types of education
— the total expenditure for books for use by prisoners in the nation's prisons for the past twenty years is less than the amount paid by the federal government for buying and dumping tens of millions of copies of technical books on air conditioning in under-developed areas of the world where there are neither electrical energy, metallurgy industries or the remotest possibilities for the types of construction that could accommodate air conditioning
— the well-conceived, well-intentioned and relatively well-subsidized modest experimental and demonstration prison education and training programs initiated by the federal government between 1964-1974 (the Golden Era of Prison Education!) reached only a few thousand prisoners of the millions in-

carcerated during that unusual decade of concern; there was hardly anything before and the cup was largely empty afterwards

— about seventy per cent of the nation's prisons and jails, of all kinds, have no educational resources at all!

The time has come, I believe, to get government out of the business of running prisons or, at a minimum, "for starters" to get government out of the business of doing anything about education in prison.

I am reminded of this scene I witnessed: It was in the Hartford City Jail, a place of confinement for over two hundred men committed for periods up to two years. The building was a short walk from the Connecticut capital and the shimmering skyscrapers of the headquarters of America's insurance, liquor and armaments businesses. The prison's "education" budget provided for a part-time education-recreation Counselor. This employee perceived his sole duty to be organizing and supervising ping-pong tournaments among the prisoners. The prison's education facilities consisted of one room, two chairs, two ping-pong paddles and one ping-pong table with net. At the time I visited there had been no ping-pong playing for about a month and the education-recreation Counselor spent his part-time at the prison in idleness. The reason, he explained: "There are no more ping-pong balls. I've requisitioned them but we've run out of money for the education budget. I'd love to bring some in on my own, but that would be contraband. I've been told to be patient."

I think that prison education can be soundly financed and prison education programs soundly operated and managed by prisoners themselves, with a little help from the outside. Here's how it would work. At any given time about two hundred thousand prisoners serving multi-year sentences and about the equivalent number serving short term sentences, or four hundred thousand in all on an annual basis, have deposited to their inmate accounts approximately five hundred dollars. The aggregate of $200,000,000 pays no interest, is not used until small amounts each week are withdrawn by prisoners for personal "approved" expenditures. I propose the establishment of a national education "money management" fund. Assuming full participation by prisoners, the fund, with $200,000,000 available on a relatively stable annual basis could yield, conservatively, about $20 million a year. The earnings would be available to prisoners as educational vouchers to be allocated for spending on educational objectives. The objectives and spending patterns would be determined by the prisoners themselves assisted by education professionals and specialists. Monies allocated for prison education by localities, counties, states and the federal government, but poorly administered, might be contributed to the education money management fund so that economies of scale could be accomplished with substantial purchasing power in volume. Governmental contributions to the fund could have the effect of increasing the rate of earnings and make still more educational voucher money available in the prisons.

Through the unified fund, it would be possible for prisons to buy into educational programming via the satellite communications system, regional high frequency telecasting, learning cassettes, teaching machines. With vouchers at their disposal prisoners might even purchase the services of teachers who have been designated as persons of outstanding ability. The availability of education vouchers in prison might motivate entrepreneurs to franchise mobile classrooms containing the latest educational technologies, equipment and materials and be in a position to deliver innovative educational resources inside prison walls.

I once visited a prison for women in the southwest. It confined almost five hundred women, all native American Indians. In virtually every instance, the cause of incarceration was an offense related to a struggle for equality before the law. Yet in spite of laws, court decisions and stated policies requiring the availability of "law books" for these women prisoners, there were none. Not even a copy of pre- as well as post-Revolution treaties between the U.S. government and various Indian nations that guaranteed Indians the integrity of their civilization, laws and lands. The situation hasn't changed very much in the southwest; the murderous riot in the Santa Fe Penitentiary a few years ago attests to the absence of a determination to carry out the laws. But with educational vouchers available, it becomes possible to buy into computerized legal research systems and obviate to a large extent the need for books and for those who know how to read them to help those who can't find the law.

For more than two centuries the promise of education for prisoners in the United States has been a boulevard of broken dreams. In a remarkable and memorable televised speech, President Lyndon B. Johnson, after speaking about how education brought him from the poverty he knew along the banks of the Pedernales River to the lofty realm of the capital, committed the nation to a formidable program of equality of education virtually without limit and for all who wanted to learn at any age. A truly vibrant, extraordinary vision. But the nation's prisoners were not included. It's time they were. And if we, on the outside, can't or won't let those on the inside do it themselves, for themselves and in doing education for themselves, they are doing good for all of us.

Sol Chaneles, PhD
Editor

Current Trends in Correctional Education: Theory and Practice

The Requirement of Restitution for Juvenile Offenders: An Alternative Disposition

Robert C. Evans
Gary D. Koederitz

ABSTRACT. A growing awareness of and concern about rapidly increasing juvenile crime rates coupled with a revitalized concern for victims have generated a disillusionment with many traditional and diversionary methods of handling juvenile offenders. Restitution is regarded by many as the most promising, logical, and effective means of achieving the dual goals of deterrence and punishment. Surveys suggest strong support for juvenile restitution and several states have recently enacted or amended juvenile restitution statutes. A review of state juvenile codes reveals that a majority of states generally permit courts to require restitution as a disposition and to determine the amount and form of reparation. A survey of juvenile court judges and probation officers representing fourteen states which permit some form of restitution revealed that about one-third of the courts require it often and two-thirds seldom or never require it. More than half regard it as an effective deterrent. Data shows that the most common form of restitution is money payments; however, there remains much disagreement as to the amount of restitution required.

Background

The traditional responses to juvenile crime are based upon the *parens parentriae* philosophy that "erring children should be protected and rehabilitated rather than subjected to the harshness of the criminal system" (President's Commission on Law Enforcement and the Administration of Justice, 1968). However, Stollery (1977)

Robert C. Evans and Gary D. Koederitz are in the Department of Criminal Justice, Louisiana State University, Shreveport, LA 71105.

noted that, even though there have been a wide variety of programs developed using traditional practices to combat juvenile crime, most have failed to reduce the problem effectively. Much of the effort has involved diversionary methods aimed at treating and rehabilitating juveniles in the community rather than subjecting them to institutionalization, and many of the diversionary programs are now coming under heavy criticisms. Martinson and Wilkes (1976) described diversionary community programs as "boy scout" models and noted that they did not achieve the success anticipated. Even though a number of different approaches have not experienced a high degree of success in reducing juvenile crime, one practice which is gaining an impressive amount of attention is restitution. Restitution is defined by Hudson and Galaway (1975) as:

> a sanction imposed by officials of the criminal justice system that requires offenders to make redress in the form of monetary or service payments to either the direct victims of the the crime or to substitute victim. In short, the concept of restitution implies the use of offender reparations as at least a part of the criminal sanction and involves some type of supervision of the repayment process by criminal justice officials. (p. 1)

Restitution is not a new concept as it has been utilized for many centuries by numerous societies; but, it has undergone major changes throughout its long history, virtually disappearing for a period in recent history (Jacob, 1975). In recent decades, there has been a renewed concern for the victim and a concomitant interest in restitution as a means of compensating the victim for injury and loss, and it is now regarded by many as an effective deterrent. Tittle (1977) outlined plans whereby restitution could be utilized to achieve punishment for offenders and compensation to victims, therefore, serving as a deterrent from future criminal acts. He suggests that restitution be required in addition to traditional penalties or in lieu of incarceration, and that restitution be derived from the offender's personal resources or from compensations from regulated labor.

Galaway (1977) contends that restitution accomplishes punishment of the offender, and at the same time, provides compensation to the victim. He outlined four basic types which would achieve these goals:

> Type I restitution involves monetary payments by the offender to the direct or actual victims of the crime.
>
> Type II restitution refers to monetary payments made by the offender to some community agency. Restitution of this type differs from a fine in that the recipient of the restitution is a charitable organization. Type II restitution is used when the victim requests that payment be made to some charity, when victim cannot be located or does not wish to participate in a restitution scheme directly, or when the victim has not experienced loss.
>
> Type III restitution requires that the offender make restitution in the form of personal services to the victim.
>
> Type IV restitution occurs when the offender is required to provide services to the community. (pp. 332-333)

Restitution programs may be implemented as a part of a sentence or as a condition of probation for non-dangerous offenders, and its use tends to involve the victim in the justice process (Galaway, 1977). Another restitution proposal would require that all offenders be imprisoned, during which time they would be provided work and be paid at current market wages, and they would remain in prison until restitution was completed and fines, if imposed, were paid (Smith, 1977).

DETERMINING THE AMOUNT OF RESTITUTION

There is little controversy in determining the amount of compensation due a victim who has suffered a harm or loss which may be equated in monetary terms. However, it becomes more difficult to assess the actual value of the resulting physical and psychological harm and the amount of restitution. Damage to or loss of properties may be estimated by determining the actual market value of restoration. But, how may damages be assessed for crimes against the person and injuries suffered by victims associated with other harms involving property offenses?

Rothbard (1977) suggests that a principle of restitution based on proportionality should be implemented whereby the offender would pay double the amount of the loss and an additional sum as compensation for associated harm, if the victim chooses. He also notes that the victim should have the option of forgiving the offender either "partially or altogether." It should be noted, however, that an exacting type of retribution system is not so easily determined for violent crimes. How, for example, does one equate the cost of life or physical injury?

Barnett (1977) suggested that it may be impractical or even impossible to devise a legal retributive/restitution system based solely upon the proportionality principle as no objective standard can be devised whereby punishments would be proportionate for the offense committed. At the same time, however, Barnett (1977) completely disregarded the proportionality principle in suggesting a "new paradigm" which incorporates a restitution plan in proportion to the crime. The "new paradigm" would necessitate a change in the way crime is viewed. A crime would be regarded as an injury to the individual rather than an offense against society. With this change of view, restitution could then be incorporated in two plans. "Punitive restitution" would be equally applied to all offenders according to the crime committed and would require the offender to compensate the victim by his own work, either in or outside prison. As he notes, however, the problem with this plan is that it is based primarily upon "the ability of the offender to pay" and not by the "harm done." The second plan is "pure restitution," a scheme whereby the focus is upon the victim rather than the offender. The goal of this plan would not be to punish the offender, but to require the offender to replenish the loss suffered by the victim. The handling of the offender during the period of restitution would be based on his trustworthiness. If, for example, an offender could be trusted to make restitution, the court would allow him to remain on his job while doing so. If he failed to make restitution, he would be "confined to an employment project," where he would remain until compensation was completed. While confined, the offender would be required to pay for room and board. This plan would also allow for direct negotiations between the convicted person and the victim for the purpose of determining the amount of restitution or length and type of services to be rendered. Barnett (1977) also recognizes the inherent problems associated with determining the amount of restitution for crimes against the person, but defends restitution, as it does provide some tangible form of compensation, however inadequate.

RESTITUTION FOR JUVENILE OFFENDERS

Society traditionally responds to juveniles' delinquent acts by placing them in the community under the supervision of a probation officer or by placing them in an institution. As noted earlier, these approaches are now being seriously questioned as effective ways of dealing with youthful offenders and of preventing future delinquent and criminal acts. During recent years the revival of restitution as an integral part of punishment for adult offenders has spurred interest in the development of juvenile restitution programs.

A recent study by Schneider, Schneider, Reiter, and Cleary (1977) involving 114 randomly selected juvenile courts throughout the country reported that restitution is utilized as one form of disposition, and that many courts have utilized restitution as a dispositional alternative for several years. Of the courts surveyed, 100 had required some form of restitution for one to more than twenty-six years. The mean number of years restitution had been used by the courts surveyed was 16.9. Juveniles, or in some instances, their families were reported to have been required to provide compensation to victims for both property and violent crimes and the determination of the amount of restitution was based on two primary considerations: the ability to pay and the loss suffered by the victim. Restitution was generally stipulated as a condition of probation and it was probation officers who most often supervised the enforcement of the restitution plan.

The changing trend toward the utilization of restitution for juveniles has been prompted, in part, by the National Advisory Committee on Criminal Justice: Standards and Goals' (1976) recommendation that:

> wages paid a delinquent should be used for payments of restitution to the victim of the offense or for purposes of contributing to the support of the delinquent's family only if so ordered by the family court as part of the disposition.[1]

In 1978, John M. Rector, Administrator of the Law Enforcement Assistance Administration's Office of Juvenile Justice and Delinquency, announced that thirty million dollars would be made avail-

---

[1]Standard 24.14, National Advisory Committee on Criminal Justice: Standards and Goals (1976).

able for the development and support of juvenile restitution programs. The purpose of establishing restitution programs were to generate a feeling of responsibility on the part of the offender and to serve as a rehabilitative tool through job placements, training and community services. Chesney, Hudson, and McLagen (1978), and Susman (1978) reported that a number of states had already passed legislation which permitted restitution for juvenile offenders. And, while the juvenile codes of some states did not specifically provide for restitution, 86% of the juvenile courts, viewed restitution as an alternative disposition (Schneider, Schneider, Reiter, & McCleary, 1977). Further, it is generally found that restitution is regarded as a condition of probation allowable under the common statutory phrase that juveniles may be placed on probation "under such conditions as the court sees fit to impose" (Chesney, Hudson, & McLagen, 1978).

There is general agreement among judges that restitution reduces recidivism among both property and personal offenders and that victims who receive compensation for their losses experience more satisfaction with the way offenders are handled by the justice system. There are also strong indications that police, judges and the community, not only favor restitution, but would support it, as well (Schneider, Schneider, Reiter, & Cleary, 1977). This same study found that the effectiveness of restitution is regarded as best under the five following conditions:

1. Direct payment to the victim rather than through an intermediary;
2. the availability of work restitution (in addition to monetary restitution);
3. the availability of community service work (in addition to monetary restitution);
4. enforcement of the restitution order by the court rather than by individual probation officers; and
5. the program goal of restitution is to benefit the youth rather than to provide compensation to the victim.

Galaway and Marsella (1976) conducted a study in which they attempted to determine the perceptions and attitudes of the various parties involved in cases requiring restitution for juveniles in St. Louis County, Minnesota. Although the number of sample cases in the study was small, the findings appeared significant. In most cases the youths, parents, victims, probation officers and police all perceived restitution as a *fair* disposition. In only 27% of the cases, the youths believed that restitution was unfair. However, while most regarded restitution as a fair disposition, there was considerable disagreement concerning the *amount* of restitution required. While most of the youthful offenders and their parents perceived the amount of restitution as a sufficient penalty, most of the victims and police perceived the amount of restitution as an insufficient penalty. Additionally, none of the probation officers believed that the amount of restitution was adequate.

PURPOSE OF THE STUDY

The purpose of this study was to determine the number of states which specifically permit juvenile restitution by statute and to secure information as to the extent to which juvenile courts require restitution as a disposition. Additional purposes were to determine the types of restitution utilized and preferred and to collect data regarding the opinions of juvenile court judges and probation officers in terms of the effectiveness of restitution as a deterrent against future delinquent actions.

METHODOLOGY

A survey was conducted of 120 juvenile court judges and probation officers in fourteen states representing four geographic regions, east, mid-west, south, and west. The officials contacted were in states with statutes specifically permitting the imposition of some form of restitution, either as one condition of a disposition, or alone as an alternative disposition. Those contacted were requested to report the frequencies of cases with which they had been directly involved during the past year that required restitution in the disposition. Additionally, they were asked to express their opinions concerning restitution as an effective disposition. Specifically, they were asked if they believed that requiring restitution functioned as an effective deterrent against future delinquent acts. The statutes of all the states were reviewed for the purposes of determining which statutes specifically permitted restitution for juvenile offenders, whether it was utilized only as a condition of probation, the types of restitution allowed or required and other relevant aspects.

ANALYSIS OF THE DATA

The results of reviewing the state statutes are presented in Table 1. While most of the states specifically provide for the imposition of restitution as a disposition for juvenile offenders, a minority of the states imply by the wording in the statutes that the court may impose those conditions which it regards as beneficial to the youth. In only one state is restitution required and that is for acts of vandalism. Some statutes provide that restitution be made in the form of monetary payments and only in the amount of the actual damage, loss, or injury. Others, however, stipulate that the court may assess the amount of restitution to be made. In addition to restitution, a number of states permit a fine, as well, but usually stipulate a ''not to exceed'' amount. Most states require that restitution be a condition of probation, but in many states, it may also be imposed in lieu of probation or other dispositions. Regardless of the type of restitution required, it is generally stipulated that it should aid in the rehabilitation and/or treatment of the youth, must be of a reasonable nature and within the abilities of the individual to perform. A common requirement among the statutes was to limit the time of involvement in a restitution program, and it was often stipulated that the restitution program could not interfere with the juvenile's schooling.

The results of the survey of juvenile court judges and probation officers are presented in Table 2. While the overall findings indicate the frequencies restitution was required are similar, the mid-west states reported that some form of restitution was required more often than other regions. In 58% of the responses, the eastern states reported that restitution was seldom required and only 19% reported it was never required. There were 50% of the respondents in the western states who reported that restitution was never required.

While only about one-half of the southern and western survey respondents were of the opinion that restitution was an effective deterrent against future delinquent behaviors, 71% of those reporting from the eastern region and 62% of those from the mid-western region believed that the requirement of some form of restitution was effective. Overall, however, 58% regarded restitution as effective; 42% did not.

The judges and probation officers were also asked to report the types of restitution required and to express their opinions as to the form they regarded as the most effective deterrent. The responses to these questions are reported in Table 3. The findings indicate that in

Table 1

Restitution Statutes by State

State and Statute	Expressly Permitted by Statute		Implied Permitted by Statute		Only as Condition of Probation		Type of Restitution			Other Aspects of Restitution Statutes
	Yes	No	Yes	No	Yes	No	Money	Public Service	Other	
ALABAMA Ala. Code Tit.28 §15-71	X					X	X			1. May impose a fine not to exceed $250.00. 2. Amount determined by court.
ALASKA Alaska Stat. §47-10-080	X					X	X			1. Court sets amount.
ARIZONA Ariz. Rev. Stat.§8-241	X				X		X			1. Court determines reasonable amount. 2. Paid in lump sum or installments.
ARKANSAS Ark. Stat. Ann.§45-436	X					X	X			1. Restitution paid to victim or to family of victim. 2. Actual amount of injury or loss.
CALIFORNIA Cal. Welfare & Institutions)§728	X				X		X	X	X	1. May be required to repair or replace damaged property. 2. Alternatively, may be required to perform community service.

Table 1-Continued

State and Statute	Expressly Permitted by Statute		Implied Permitted by Statute		Only as Condition of Probation		Type of Restitution			Other Aspects of Restitution Statutes
	Yes	No	Yes	No	Yes	No	Money	Public Service	Other	
COLORADO Col. Rev. Stat. §19-3-112	X				X		X			1. Maximum 180 day work program.
CONNECTICUT Conn.Gen. Stat. §466-140	X					X	X	X		1. May be in lieu of adjudication. 2. Fine of $1000.00 allowed.
DELAWARE Del.Code Tit. 10 §926-937	X					X	X			1. Court may require parent or child to make restitution up to $5,000.00.
FLORIDA Fla. Stat. Ann. §39.11	X				X			X		1. Child not entitled to benefits of work program.
GEORGIA Ga.Code Ann. §24A-2302		X	X		X		X	X		1. Restitution not to exceed actual damage.
HAWAII Haw.Rev. Stat. Tit. 31 §571-48	X					X	X		X	1. Permits a fine. 2. May require service to the victim.

Table 1-Continued

State and Statute	Expressly Permitted by Statute		Implied Permitted by Statute		Only as Condition of Probation		Type of Restitution			Other Aspects of Restitution Statutes
	Yes	No	Yes	No	Yes	No	Money	Public Service	Other	
IDAHO Idaho Code §16-1814	X					X	X	X	X	1. Full or partial restitution in the manner prescribed by court.
ILLINOIS Ill. Ann. Stat. Ch. 37 §705-3		X		X						
INDIANA Ind. Code Ann. §31-6-4-16	X				X		X			
IOWA Iowa Code §232.34	X					X	X	X		1. May be alone or part of other dispositions.
KANSAS Kan. Stat. §38-826		X	X				X			1. Fine of $150.00 for each offense allowed.
KENTUCKY Ky. Rev. Stat. Ann. §208.240	X					X	X			1. Sum and conditions determined by court.
LOUISIANA La. Code Crim. Pro. Ann. Art. 83	X				X				X	1. Form of restitution not specified.

Table 1-Continued

State and Statute	Expressly Permitted by Statute		Implied Permitted by Statute		Only as Condition of Probation		Type of Restitution			Other Aspects of Restitution Statutes
	Yes	No	Yes	No	Yes	No	Money	Public Service	Other	
MAINE Me.Rev.Stat. Tit. 507 §33.14	X				X		X	X	X	1. May be required to work for the victim. 2. Court determines amount. 3. Work program cannot exceed 180 days.
MARYLAND (Court & Judicial Proceedings) Code Ann. §3820	X					X	X			1. Restitution may be imposed on parents or guardian as well.
MASSACHUSETTS Mass.Ann.Laws Ch. 119 §62	X				X		X			
MICHIGAN Mich.Stat. Ann. §712. A18		X	X			X				
MINNESOTA Minn.Stat. §260.185	X				X		X			1. Property damage only
MISSISSIPPI Miss.Code Ann. §43-21-605	X				X		X	X	X	1. Fines are allowed, not to exceed $300.00. 2. Restitution may be performed through services to the victim.

Table 1-Continued

State and Statute	Expressly Permitted by Statute: Yes	Expressly Permitted by Statute: No	Implied Permitted by Statute: Yes	Implied Permitted by Statute: No	Only as Condition of Probation: Yes	Only as Condition of Probation: No	Type of Restitution: Money	Type of Restitution: Public Service	Type of Restitution: Other	Other Aspects of Restitution Statutes
MISSOURI Mo.Ann.Stat. §211.181	X				X		X	X		1. Based on child's ability to make payment or perform reparation.
MONTANA Mont.Rev.Codes Ann. §41-5-523	X					X	X			1. Court determines amount.
NEBRASKA Neb.Rev.Stat. §43-210	X				X		X			1. Restitution may be ordered for property damaged or stolen.
NEVADA Nev.Rev.Stat. tit.5 §62.200		X	X							
NEW HAMPSHIRE N.H.Rev.Stat. Ann. §169-B:19	X					X	X			1. Fines may also be imposed, not to exceed $250.00.
NEW JERSEY N.J.Stat.Ann. §2A:4-61		X	X		X		X			1. Fine is allowed. 2. May not be institutionalized nor probation revoked for failure to pay.
NEW MEXICO N.M.Stat.Ann. §32-1-34		X	X			X	X			1. The court has expansive authority in determining conditions of probation.

Table 1 -Continued

State and Statute	Expressly Permitted by Statute		Implied Permitted by Statute		Only as Condition of Probation		Type of Restitution			Other Aspects of Restitution Statutes
	Yes	No	Yes	No	Yes	No	Money	Public Service	Other	
NEW YORK N.Y. (N.Y. Family Court Act) Law §757 (McKinney)	X				X		X	X	X	1. Property offenses only. 2. Services without pay may be required.
NO. CAROLINA N.C.Gen.Stat. §7A-286		X	X				X		X	
NO. DAKOTA N.D.Cent.Code §27-20-31		X		X					X	
OHIO Ohio Rev.Code Ann. §2151.355	X					X	X			1. If child's victim was 65 years of age or older, this fact is in favor of imposing restitution. 2. Fines not to exceed $50.00.
OKLAHOMA Okla.Stat.tit. 10 §114.6	X					X	X	X	X	1. May require work on public, civil or charitable projects, not to exceed 6 weeks.
OREGON Or.Rev.Stat. §419.507 §419.630	X					X				1. May be community service. 2. May be an informal disposition.
PENNSYLVANIA 11 Pa.Cons. Stat.§2003-2004		X		X						1. Court may direct parents to make payment not to exceed $300.00 for the delinquent act of child.

Table 1 -Continued

State and Statute	Expressly Permitted by Statute: Yes	Expressly Permitted by Statute: No	Implied Permitted by Statute: Yes	Implied Permitted by Statute: No	Only as Condition of Probation: Yes	Only as Condition of Probation: No	Type of Restitution: Money	Type of Restitution: Public Service	Type of Restitution: Other	Other Aspects of Restitution Statutes
RHODE ISLAND R.I.Gen.Laws §14-1-32, and §14-1-32.1	X					X	X	X		1. Amount set by court. 2. If parents make restitution, child may be required to perform community service.
SO.CAROLINA S.C.Code §15-1412	X				X		X			1. Actual damage or loss paid to victim.
SO.DAKOTA S.D.Compiled Laws Ann. §26-8-40.1	X					X	X		X	1. May be supervised work program with no pay. 2. Property damage only. 3. Fine not to exceed $50.00.
TENNESSEE Tenn.Code Ann. §37-231		X	X							1. Restitution impliedly permitted. 2. Fine not to exceed $50.00 permitted
TEXAS Tex.Fam.Code Ann.tit. 54 §.04 (Vernon)	X					X				1. Property damage only. 2. May perform personal services to charitable or educational institutions if unable to pay.
UTAH Utah Code Ann §78-3a-99	X					X	X			1. May be encouraged to participate in work programs to fulfill obligations of restitution. 2. May impose reasonable fine.
VERMONT Vt.Stat.Ann. tit.33§657		X	X							

Table 1 -Continued

State and Statute	Expressly Permitted by Statute		Implied Permitted by Statute		Only as Condition of Probation		Type of Restitution			Other Aspects of Restitution Statutes
	Yes	No	Yes	No	Yes	No	Money	Public Service	Other	
Virginia Va. Code §16.1-279	X					X				1. For actual loss or damage.
Washington Wash. Rev. Code Ann. §13.40·190	X					X	X			1. Required when offense caused loss or damage.
West Virginia W. Va. Code §49-5-13		X	X				X			1. Informal adjustments allowed upon counsel and advice of probation officer.
Wisconsin Wis.Stat. Ann. §49.34	X					X	X	X		1. Restitution only for actual damage or injury, excluding pain and suffering. 2. May impose a fine of $50.00.
Wyoming Wyo. Stat. §14-6-229	X					X	X			1. May be required to participate in a community service project. 2. Fine is allowed and paid to the county public school fund.

Table 2

Dispositions Requiring Restitution and Opinions of Juvenile Judges and Probation Officers on Effectiveness

			Frequencies of Dispositions Requiring Restitution			Opinions on Restitution as Effective	
Region	State	N Surveyed	Often	Seldom	Never	Yes	No
East	Mass.	10	3	7	0	5	5
	N.J.	10	1	7	2	6	4
	R.I.	6	2	1	3	5	1
	Totals	26	6=23%	15=58%	5=19%	16=62%	10=38%
Mid-West	Minn.	8	8	0	0	8	0
	Mo.	10	2	4	4	5	5
	Neb.	6	1	3	2	4	2
	Ohio	11	6	1	4	8	3
	Totals	35	17=48%	8=23%	10=29%	25=71%	10=29%
South	Ark.	9	3	4	2	6	3
	La.	12	2	3	7	4	8
	Miss.	10	4	2	4	5	5
	Totals	31	9=29%	9=29%	13=42%	15=48%	16=52%
West	Ariz.	8	3	0	5	4	4
	Calif.	8	4	2	2	6	2
	Colo.	7	2	2	3	3	4
	N.M.	5	0	1	4	1	4
	Totals	28	9=32%	5=18%	14=50%	14=50%	14=50%
Totals	N=	120	41=34%	37=31%	42=35%	70=58%	50=42%

Table 3

Types of Restitution Required and Juvenile Judges and Probation Officers' Opinions on

Most Effective Forms-By Region

		Type of Restitution Required						Most Effective Form					
		Money		Public Service		Work for Victim		Money		Public Service		Work for Victim	
Region	N	N	%	N	%	N	%	N	%	N	%	N	%
East	26	18	69	6	23	2	8	18	69	3	12	5	19
Mid-west	35	20	57	7	20	8	23	22	63	5	14	8	23
South	31	22	71	6	19	3	10	19	61	5	16	7	23
West	28	17	57	9	30	4	13	15	50	5	17	10	33
Totals	N=120	77	64%	28	23%	17	14%	74	62%	18	15%	30	25%

Percentages may not toal 100 due to rounding.

all regions the most preferred restitution form is the payment of money, as opposed to public/community service or requiring the offender to work for the victim. An interesting finding was that 14% reported requiring the offender to work for the victim, and 25% were of the opinion that if proper supervision could be provided, it would be preferable to have the juvenile work for or perform some direct service for the victim.

CONCLUSIONS

In reviewing the literature, state statutes and the findings of this survey, there seems to be little remaining doubt that requiring juveniles to make some form of restitution is gaining support as an effective dispositional alternative for handling juvenile offenders. And, while the long-term effects on the prevention of future delinquent, and criminal acts are uncertain, the prospects appear promising. Not only is restitution highly regarded and supported by government as evidenced by funds allocated for restitution programs and by recently passed legislation permitting restitution for juveniles, but most juvenile justice practitioners indicate strong support for and favorable attitude toward restitution as an effective and appropriate dispositional alternative, as well.

It should be noted also that in terms of cost effectiveness, restitution seems even more feasible in that it provides, at least, some tangible recompense to the victims, of juvenile crime and promotes victim's involvement in the justice process.

Victims' involvement in the justice processes would be further realized if more juveniles were required to perform any one or several direct services to the victim. It should be noted, however, that direct services to the victim would necessitate a thorough screening process so as to exclude violent or potentially dangerous offenders. It would seem that the most obvious candidates for performing direct services would be those who have committed property offenses.

REFERENCES

Barnett, R. E. Restitution: A new paradigm of criminal justice. In R. Barnett & J. Hagel, III (Eds.), *Assessing the criminal: Restitution, retribution, and the legal process.* Cambridge, Mass.: Ballinger Publishing Company, 1977.

Chesney, S. L., Hudson, B., & McLagen, J. A new look at restitution: Recent legislation. *Judicature,* 1978, *61*(48), 348-357.

Galaway, B. Restitution as an integrative punishment. In R. Barnett, & J. Hagel, III (Eds.), *Assessing the criminal: restitution, retribution, and the legal process.* Cambridge, Mass.: Ballinger Publishing Company, 1977.

Galaway, B., & Marsella, W. *An exploratory study of the perceived fairness of restitution as a sanction for juvenile offenders.* Paper presented at the Second International Symposium on Victimology, Boston, Mass., September, 1976.

Hudson, J., & Galaway, B. (Eds.), *Restitution in criminal justice.* Lexington, Mass.: Lexington Books, 1975.

Jacob, J. R. The concept of restitution. In J. Hudson & B. Galaway (Eds.), *Restitution in criminal justice.* Lexington, Mass.: Lexington Books, 1975.

Martinson, R. & Wilkes, J. Is the treatment of criminal offenders really necessary? *Federal Probation, 40*(1), 1976, 3-9.

National Advisory Committee on Criminal Justice: *Standards and Goals.* Washington, D.C.: United States Printing Office, 1976.

President's Commission on Law Enforcement and the Administration of Justice. *The challenge of crime in a free society.* Washington, D.C.: U.S. Government Printing Office, 1968.

Rector announces LEAA restitution funding. *Juvenile justice digest, 65*(March 3), 1978, 2-3.

Rothbard, M. N. Punishment and proportionality. In R. Barnett & H. Hagel, III (Eds.), *Assessing the criminal: Restitution, retribution, and the legal process,* Cambridge, Mass.: Ballinger Publishing Company, 1977.

Schneider, P. R., Schneider, A. L., Reiter, P. D., & Cleary, C. M. Restitution requirements for juvenile offenders: a survey of the practices in American juvenile courts. *Juvenile justice, 28*(4), 1977, 43-56.

Smith, K. Implementing restitution within a penal setting: the case for a self-determinate sentence. In J. Hudson and B. Galaway (Eds.), *Restitution in criminal justice.* Lexington, Mass.: Lexington Books, 1975.

Stollery, P. L. Searching for the magic answer to juvenile delinquency. *Federal probation, 41*(4), 1977.

Susman, A. Changes in juvenile law and procedure. *Criminal law bulletin, 14*(4), 1978, 311-342.

Tittle, C. R. Restitution and deterrence: An evaluation of compatability. In J. Hudson & B. Galaway (Eds.), *Offender restitution in theory and action.* Lexington, Mass.: Lexington Books, 1977.

Content and Process of Detention Education

David W. Roush

ABSTRACT. A call for quality correctional education programs has been voiced by leading federal officials. While focused on adult programs, efforts to upgrade correctional education programs will inevitably benefit juvenile offenders. Within this context, educational programs in juvenile detention facilities are in need of greater definition. Renewed emphasis on juvenile correctional education has revealed an accumulation of relevant information. When combined with experiences in an effective detention education program, a model for the content and process of detention education programming is presented.

The current emphasis on standards for juvenile offender programs has resulted from the increased demand for accountability and quality programming for juveniles (Kehoe, 1980). Within the area of juvenile detention services, the establishment of minimum standards has served to create workable guidelines for quality programs. One area, however, has not received adequate attention. Detention education programs continue to be one of the most ill-defined areas of detention services. The Commission on Accreditation for Correction (1979) presents a basic minimum defintion of a detention education program. As a component of the total detention services, detention education programs are designed to (a) keep the student current with his/her studies in the public school, (b) provide remedial education for those students with special education concerns, (c) incor-

---

David W. Roush is the director of the Calhoun County Juvenile Home, a division of the Calhoun County Juvenile Court. He is currently the president of the Michigan Juvenile Detention Association.

Requests for reprints may be addressed to the author at Calhoun County Juvenile Home, 14555 18½ Mile Road, Marshall, MI 49068.

porate specialized educational equipment which meet the minimum state educational standards.

Detention education has received inadequate attention due, in part, to the fact that (a) detention programs constitute such a small portion of the criminal justice system and (b) detention education programs constitute an equally small part of the educational systems. For example, while there are approximately 400 detention homes in the United States (Hughes & Reuterman, 1980), this figure constitutes less than 7% of the correctional institutions in the United States. Subsequently, relevant information about education programs within institutions has been generated by correctional education personnel.

Leadership in correctional education has benefited detention education programs. There are, however, two major distinctions between correctional educational programs and detention education programs. First, the administration of these educational programs is different. Within the state correctional systems, a division of education constitutes the administrative staff. Whereas, detention education programs are usually administered by a separate school board or agency. Thus, detention educators are not supervised by the detention administrator. Second, the length of stay in a detention education program is considerably less than the length of stay in a correctional education program. Other than these two basic differences, the goals and objectives of correctional education and detention education are very similar. Since correctional educators have been more active in defining and upgrading their profession, detention educators have been able to apply these advances to detention education program.

There is a special concern in the field of correctional education which is directly relevant to detention education. Students with exceptional needs constitute a considerable proportion of the institutional population. Even though the figures range from 21% to 90% (Murray, 1976; Prout, 1981; Smith, Wydra, & Klotz, 1981), there is little doubt in the minds of correctional educators that special education programs are needed for a sizable number of the students. For this reason, detention education programs have traditionally been included under the special education programming for state and local school districts. Furthermore, the special needs presented by these students require detention education programs that are responsive and comprehensive in their approach.

Dissatisfied with the attention given detention education, the Michigan Juvenile Detention Association (MJDA) generated a forum for detention educators to express their concerns for more effective detention education programs (Roush & Morris, 1980). Based on an analysis of these issues, detention educators, detention administrators, and detention school coordinators were asked to prepare a list of priorities for detention education. Morris (1980) reports the following list of priorities for detention education in Michigan:

1. Each student should have a comprehensive set of educational goals which culminate in an aftercare plan.
2. Improved communication systems are needed between detention education staff and court staff, detention staff, parents, other facilities, and students.
3. Detention education curriculum should include substance abuse and mental health programming, GED information, vocational training, treatment components, survival skills, and coping skills.
4. There is a need for increased information regarding rules and regulations from state and federal sources and GED information. Additionally, the label of emotionally impaired or emotionally disturbed should be removed from the classification of detention education students. Finally, rules and regulations should specify that an in-house education director be assigned to each detention education program.
5. There is a need for coordinated program goals between education staff and detention staff.

This process also identified several problems for detention education. Specifically, detention education is viewed by practitioners as a process which is larger than the minimal definitions cited above. Additional problems have resulted from the dual administration of detention facilities and detention education programs. The frequent lack of continuity between detention programs and detention education programs has generated both a confusion surrounding professional identity and a low priority status of detention educators within special education organizations.

Renewed emphasis on detention education poses several interesting questions. The purpose of this paper is to attempt to answer these questions regarding the content and process of detention education. For example, who should provide the direct services for detention education? What should be taught in detention education programs? Finally, how does an effective detention education program operate?

ACCEPTABLE STANDARDS

Investigation into the detention education process is not a new concern. Through the pioneering work of Norman (1960), a body of information exists which can constitute the foundation of a detention education program. Additional studies by Hughes (1972), Duran (1979), and Hughes and Reuterman (1980) provide workable data on detention education programs. As a result of these efforts, the following are acceptable minimum standards for the organization of detention education programs which exceed those standards recommended by the Commission on Accreditation for Corrections (1979):

(1) It is generally accepted that detention education programs should be administered by separate board of education which is distinct from the administering agency for the detention facility. This concept of a separate administration was recommended by Norman over 20 years ago. In a recent national survey of juvenile detention facilities, Hughes and Reuterman report that over 72% of all detention education programs are administered by a separate board or agency.

(2) Recognizing the need to serve the exceptional children in detention facilities, Duran recommends that teacher qualifications for detention education include a minimum of a special education certificate. Again, this appears to be a generally accepted practice; however, questions have arisen about the relevance of educational programs for special education teachers. The debate centers more around the content of special education training than around the usefulness of a special education teacher in a detention education program.

(3) Norman and Duran recommend that a detention education program operate on a 52-week basis. This recommendation has not been widely accepted due to conflicts with teacher contracts. Several alternatives have been attempted in order to lengthen the duration of the detention education program. For example, some institutions stagger the contract for various teachers so that a program is operating for the entire year. These efforts appear to have had some

success in lengthening the school year for detention education programs. Hughes and Reuterman report that the average duration of a detention education program is 43 weeks. While this average falls short of the ideal 52-week program, it does exceed the normal 36-week program in the public schools.

(4) There is general consensus that the class size for detention education programs should be small. Both Norman and Duran recommend a class size of 10 students per teacher. Norman specifically recommends that there should be no more than five students per class when teaching remedial subjects.

(5) Finally, generally accepted minimum standards call for the maintenance of education files that are separate and apart from the resident filing system within the detention facility.

To develop a model detention education program, attention must be given to the issues of the detention educator, the detention education curriculum, and an effective implementation strategy. The basic standards cited above provide a foundation from which to build the content of a detention education program. Additionally, the MJDA survey (Morris, 1980) provides greater focus on the extent of the problems facing detention education. Therefore, the following sections shall attempt to answer the questions of who, what, and how.

DETENTION EDUCATOR

Clearly, one of the most important elements in a successful detention education program is the detention educator. Yet, with so little agreement on the standards for detention education, it is often difficult to define the purpose of the detention educator. Again, reference is made to insights from 30 years ago. In 1949, John Costello (in Duran, 1979) set forth a purpose for the detention educator when he stated:

> Teachers in schools for delinquents must be persons who can be comfortable working with the public school failures. They must be able to accept the fact that their students are retarded (that is, culturally and educationally) and their job is to try to rebuild in the pupil confidence in his ability to learn. (p. 6)

It appears reasonable to conclude that if the detention educator does nothing more than rebuild the student's confidence in his/her ability to learn, then the detention education process has been a success.

Using this purpose for the detention educator, what are the necessary traits and abilities required to accomplish this goal? Duran (1979) addresses this issue and outlines four essential traits and abilities: (a) flexibility, (b) patience, (c) ability to teach subject matter, and (d) ability to work with others. Referenced as highly desirable traits and abilities are: (e) creativity, (f) empathy, and (g) diagnostic ability. Representing the views of detention educators, these traits and abilities constitute a basis for personnel recruitment and evaluation.

Ideally, these characteristics of the detention educator are generated through the teacher education programs within special education departments at colleges and universities. However, the teacher education process has recently come under severe criticism. Therefore, it is reasonable to ask whether or not the teacher education process needs redefinition. Because detention education constitutes such a small portion of the special education process, greater clarity of purpose could provide useful information to educators in the teacher education systems.

Bowen (1981) outlines two components of the educational process for correctional educators. He asserts that the purpose of teacher education is to (a) provide specific clinical teaching skills, and (b) provide behavior management skills. This definition emphasizes the two critical components raised in the MJDA survey—teaching skills and treatment skills. Recognizing this need for a more interdisciplinary educational process, the Starr Commonwealth Schools (Note 1), in conjunction with the Ohio State and Western Michigan Universities, have initiated the educatuer masters degree program which incorporates coursework from the special education, recreation, child development, and social work disciplines. Because it so directly addresses the issues of teaching and treatment skills, the educatuer program warrants additional consideration as an acceptable educational prerequisite for the detention educator.

After addressing those qualities that a detention educator should ideally bring to the job and after defining the purpose of teacher education, what are the skills or competencies required for the detention educator? Bowen (1981) has generated a list of 10 competencies for correctional educators based on his work with teacher inservice education programs. These competencies are as follows:

1. Given student background information data, the teacher can

select and administer a battery of diagnostic tests to identify assets and deficits in academic content areas.

2. Given a profile of student strengths and weaknesses in general achievement and academic content areas, the teacher can write a set of long- and short-range instructional objectives.
3. Given a profile of student strengths and weaknesses in general achievement and content areas, the teacher can write specific, clinical teaching plans in such academic context areas as reading, language, mathematics, government, spelling, science, and driver education.
4. Given a . . . student having deficits in major academic learning skill areas, the teacher can demonstrate the use of alternative teaching methods and strategies in direct teaching.
5. Given a direct teaching setting, the teacher can evaluate a teaching plan for student skill development and revise the plan to correct deficiencies.
6. Given a direct teaching setting, the teacher can demonstrate appropriate application of supplementary instructional materials and media.
7. Given a direct teaching setting, the teacher can demonstrate the integration of counseling skills, behavior management, and recordkeeping.
8. Given student performance data, the teacher can summarize the student skills and present the summary of performance in a written report and staffing conference with selected institution and/or school personnel.
9. Given an objective (academic/maladaptive behavior), the teacher can write a task analysis of and adapt a set of assigned materials to match the student's skill level.
10. Given a set of legal/instructional terms, the teacher can demonstrate knowledge of the terms as they apply to treatment programs for adjudicated youth. (p. 15)

CURRICULUM

There is very little debate over curricula for detention education programs. Practitioners generally agree that the primary purposes of a detention education curriculum are to keep the student current with his/her studies in public schools and to provide remedial instruction when needed. Since most detention education programs have received an adequate amount of staff and resources to expand this curriculum concept, controversy has emerged as to how sophisticated a detention education curriculum should become.

Brown and Robbins (1981) outline five general areas for curriculum development in a correctional education setting. These general areas are (a) GED preparation and information, (b) vocational awareness and training, (c) survival skills, (d) remedial instruction, and (e) general academic programming. The concentration of effort in any of these particular areas is a function of the educational philosophy of the particular detention education staff. Based on a survey of current practices, Duran (1979) reports the following areas for detention education curriculum:

1. Math
2. Remedial Math
3. Remedial Reading
4. Arts and Crafts
5. Guidance
6. Physical Education
7. Social Studies
8. GED Preparation (p. 27)

Additional curriculum included vocational education, career education, health, sex education, job interview skills, consumer education skills, and science. When compared with the five general areas cited by Brown and Robbins, Duran's curriculum issues fall into each of the five categories.

Comparing these curriculum issues with the MJDA survey (Morris, 1981), there appears to be a general sense of satisfaction with the level of programming in the general academic and remedial subject areas. Detention educators in Michigan view GED preparation, vocational education, and survival skills as priority issues for continued development. Moreover, Morris and Duran both report a growing emphasis by detention educators on treatment/guidance services through the detention education program.

OBSTACLES TO IMPLEMENTATION

To implement a successful detention education program, there must be cooperation between detention educators and the detention staff. Because each group is administered by a separate agency, cooperation has the potential of being extremely difficult to accomplish. When reporting unique elements of detention education programs, Duran (1979) cites only one program where mutual cooperation between detention educators and detention staff is listed as a primary factor in the success of the detention education program. Based on the author's experience in that program, several inherent obstacles to efficient implementation of a detention education program have been identified. By realizing that these problems exist, efforts were made to reduce the adverse impact they had on generating a team approach to detention education.

Credentials

The credentials that staff bring to the detention environment can create a source of conflict. While there is little evidence to support the notion of a direct relationship between competent job performance and education, many people are resistant to input, suggestions, or constructive criticism from co-workers who have a lesser educational background. This educational disparity frequently occurs in detention settings. For example, Norde (1977) reports that 71% of the correctional educators nationally possess a bachelor's degree. Whereas, Hughes and Reuterman (1980) report that only 50% of all detention personnel possess a minimum of a bachelor's degree. These same studies reveal educational disparity at the master's level with 28% of correctional educators possessing a master's degree while only 11% of detention personnel possess a master's degree. With increasing emphasis on graduate education, it is reasonable to assume that the percentages cited by Norde have increased since the time of his survey. In Michigan, however, the disparity at the master's level does not appear to be as great an issue. Roush (1981) reports that 43% of all program staff in Michigan's detention facilities possess a minimum of a master's degree.

A second concern relates to the amount of experience each staff member brings to the job. In most cases, detention educators have more experience in teaching than child care workers have in detention services. Again, while increased experience does not guarantee better job performance, there is a tendency to disregard the input and evaluation from newer staff members. Due to the high rate of turn-over in detention facilities, the disparity between the amount of experience for detention educators and line staff presents an ongoing problem.

Salary

Based on similar qualifications, detention educators are usually better paid than detention workers. While a basic parity at the starting rate exists in many states, pay ranges for detention educators usually include a greater number of increments. Stipulations in the teaching contract often include educational incentives and increments. Additionally, teacher benefits usually exceed those benefits provided to detention workers. While a person's worth is not measured by the amount of money he/she makes, the possibility of resentment exists when salary comparisons are treated lightly.

Work Schedule

It is often difficult for detention workers to reconcile the fact that their involvement in an offender's life is equally as important as the detention educator's involvement when detention educators make more money *and* work fewer hours. Generally, the detention educator's work day includes five to six hours on the job while the detention worker is responsible for an eight-hour shift. Furthermore, detention educators work approximately 188 days per year while the detention worker logs 261 days per year.

Vacation schedules present another concern. While detention educators will argue that their days off on vacation and holidays are unpaid, most detention workers concede that the stress of detention work makes time off a valuable commodity. Because detention facilities are in operation 24 hours a day, seven days a week, the ability to spend holidays with family and friends takes a high priority. If this issue is treated casually, conflict will inevitably occur.

Approach

When the detention education program is separated from the detention program with little or no support for interaction, both staffs tend to make assumptions about the other's job through second-hand information. When this occurs, it is common that detention educators and detention line workers hold differing philosophies about their purpose in the detention setting. The differences in these philosophies becomes most pronounced in the approach taken to working with detention residents.

From the perspective of the detention educator, some commonly held assumptions are that teachers are better therapists; real treatment or behavior change actually occurs in the detention education program; and detention workers are more concerned with control and suppression of behavior. Conversely, detention workers often assume that teachers are naive, inconsistent, too easily manipulated, a security risk, and too "feelings" oriented; teachers are hired to teach and not to do therapy; teachers do not respect the detention worker's skills; and teachers do not understand institutional treatment. When administrators allow these assumptions to become commonplace, open conflict often exists between detention educators and detention workers. Moreover, both programs become isolated and little, if any, consistency exists between programs.

Supervision

In many detention facilities, a double standard exists for staff. For example, detention workers are required to follow certain procedural guidelines relating to safety and security for residents. In most institutions, line workers are held accountable through disciplinary action for gross errors in compliance with work rules. Because detention educators are administered by a separate agency, the possibility exists that the work rules for detention educators are less stringent than those for the detention worker. Additionally, many detention educators do not receive direct supervision from their administering agency. It is also common to find detention educators uninformed about policy and procedural issues for their particular detention setting.

As long as the concept of separate administering agencies exists for detention education programming, there must be a cooperative agreement between the detention education agency and the detention facility to coordinate work rules and accountability. Without this type of collaborative effort, consistency between programs will be difficult to accomplish.

Contract

Attempting to overcome the obstacles presented by dual administration is difficult enough without adding other confounding variables. However, the teaching contract for detention educators presents another variable which tends to compound the problems of detention education. In fact, very few teacher contracts include special clauses that address the concerns of detention education programs.

Contract-generated conflicts usually involve an inflexible response to problem-solving. Primarily oriented to the public school situation, teacher contracts prescribe the hours in the work day, the yearly school schedule, teacher qualifications, and job duties. Contracts rarely take into account the fact that detention facilities detain residents during the entire year. Subsequently, the summer months present an opportunity for remedial instruction that has not been fully used, and this is only one example where teacher contracts do not convey a flexibility which would express concern for the best interests of the detained youth.

The process of resolving these obstacles to an effective detention education program is contingent upon mutual agreement on the locus of control, institutional goals, and teamwork. Because detention is a function of the judicial process, problems can be reduced by acknowledging those expectations placed upon detention programs through state regulations, juvenile law, and specific demands of each individual court jurisdiction. Ultimately, it is the juvenile court that bears final responsibility for the quantity and quality of services provided to a juvenile during his/her stay in a detention facility. Therefore, both the detention and the detention education programs must coordinate efforts to provide a maximally effective intervention. To accomplish this goal, detention education programs must complement the programs operated in the detention facility. Brown and Robbins (1981) state:

> In order for these kinds of programs to be carried out most effectively within the institutional community, it is essential that they be developed in conjunction with the counseling services in the institutional approach to treatment or therapy. (p. 13)

To generate a consistent program, a mutually agreeable goal is helpful. Therefore, benefit can be derived by starting from the assumption that the purpose of a detention facility is to provide rehabilitative services for all detained youth. Secondly, education must be viewed as a vital component of the rehabilitative effort. Using a simple conceptualization, rehabilitation focuses on personal, social, and educational development. However, there is considerable interaction between each of these areas such that a rigid compartmentalizing would be counterproductive. By clearly establishing legal parameters and a mutually agreeable goal, the groundwork is set for collaborative efforts between detention educators and detention staff.

TEAM CONCEPT

Teamwork is the commonly recommended strategy for educational programming in an institutional setting (Amos & Manella, 1966; Anderson, 1981; Prout, 1981). However, teamwork cannot be taken lightly. Many detention administrators falsely assume that cooperation and communication between detention staff and detention educators constitutes the teaming process. Effective teamwork is based on a mutual respect among members. Using the team building format recommended by Roush and Steelman (1981), education must be included as a component of the teaming network.

One example of an effective teaming effort provides partnerships for all elements of the detention program. Staff from counseling, education, group living, and recreation meet in a weekly team session to evaluate each resident assigned to the team. Ongoing monitoring of treatment objectives include detention educators' comments and recommendations. Special educational concerns are often referred to line staff for additional instruction and/or supervised homework in the evenings and on weekends.

This arrangement helps to reduce the arbitrary distinctions created by job titles. All staff may view themselves as a vital component in a youth's rehabilitation. In particular, educators are drawn into the treatment processes and given responsibilities based on their strengths. This total interfacing enables the team concept to become effective because of the sharing of direct service responsibilities based on a recognition of mutual strengths.

The momentum of successful teaming can be sustained through in-service training. Detention educators should be included in both preservice and in-service training programs (Brown & Robbins, 1981). Additionally, detention educators should be given the opportunity to present in-service sessions on detention education concepts and programs. Through the training process, administrators can provide an ongoing exchange of ideas and opinions between detention staff and detention educators. Experience has indicated that this process enables both staff to realize the importance of working together for the best interest of the detained youth.

IMPLICATIONS

A cooperative relationship between detention staff and detention educators can demonstrate benefits in numerous program areas. Perhaps the greatest advantage is the opportunity to increase program effectiveness. For example, Kilty (Note 2) and Goodrich (1981) report significant gains in reading by students in a detention facility where an effective team concept operates. Moreover, program effectiveness may be enhanced through teamwork by allowing for an expansion in the detention education curriculum. Since most detention staff include workers who hold valid teaching certificates, educational programs may be expanded by the use of certified line staff during non-school hours and qualify as legitimate coursework through supervision by the detention education coordinator. Specific examples include, but are not limited to: (a) physical education, (b) art, (c) industrial arts, (d) vocational/career development, and (e) personal adjustment. When this type of arrangement occurs, detention educators have additional time to expand the curriculum and service more students. Through teamwork, creative programming can become a reality, and the ultimate benefactor is the detained resident.

Additional advantages of teamwork are noted through increased program consistency, increased staff involvement, and increased job satisfaction. Further, by incorporating detention education into the inservice training program for the detention facility, a greater understanding and sharing between staff is provided. The direct effect of this process is to reduce the significance of those obstacles to successful implementation of a detention education program cited above. Perhaps one of the greatest advantages cannot be realized until a student is released from the detention facility. Because the vast majority of detained youth return to the community through the public schools, the importance of an effective detention education program cannot be overemphasized. In fact, Wolford (1980) states that education may be one of the most effective transitions between the institution and the community.

Detention programs are unique. Although frequently criticized, detention remains an integral part of the juvenile justice system. Therefore, to maximize the benefit of detention program, administrators must develop effective programs for short-term rehabilitation. Education is one of the most important components in this rehabilitative process. Thus, detention education programs must be developed and integrated into the total detention process. When successfully integrated, detention educators become oriented to short-term intervention strategies. This realization better enables detention educators to provide effective teaching in a limited period of time.

Although inherent problems exist in detention services, creative solutions are feasible within the detention community. Collaborative efforts between detention educators and detention staff have demonstrated an increased program effectiveness for detained youth. However, a collaborative effort requires a commitment to change on the part of *all* detention personnel. In the final analysis, this cooperation between all elements of detention services may be the major challenge for detention programs in the 1980s.

REFERENCE NOTES

1. For more information on the educatuer program, contact: Mr. Arlin Ness, President, Starr Commonwealth Schools, Albion, Michigan 49224.
2. Kilty, T. K. Teaching reading to inmates . . . successfully. Paper presented at the International Conference of the Correctional Education Association, Los Angeles, July 1981.

REFERENCES

Amos, W., & Manella, R. *Delinquent children in juvenile correctional institutions.* Springfield, IL: Thomas, 1966.

Anderson, D. An assessment of vocational programs in Illinois' juvenile and adult correctional facilities. *Journal of Correctional Education,* 1981, *32,* 16-19.

Bowen, M. Preparing correctional educators to teach delinquents with learning and reading disabilities. *Journal of Correctional Education,* 1981, *33,* 15-16.

Brown, S., & Robbins, M. Serving the special education needs of students in correctional facilities. *Journal of Correctional Education,* 1981, *33,* 11-14.

Commission on Accreditation for Corrections. *Manual of standards for juvenile detention facilities and services.* Rockville, MD: American Correctional Association, 1979.

Duran, P. *A model education program for juvenile detention homes in the United States.* Sarasota: University of Sarasota, 1979. (ERIC Document Reproduction Service No. ED 184 048)

Goodrich, R. Title I funds at work: One program's description. *Together,* 1981, Spring, 7-8.

Hughes, T. A study of the educational programs that exist for juveniles detained in detention homes in the United States. (Doctoral dissertation, St. Louis University, 1972). *Dissertation Abstracts International,* 1972, *34,* 08A-4871. (University Microfilms No. GAX74-04526)

Hughes, T., & Reuterman, N. *A national survey of juvenile detention facilities.* Edwardsville, IL: Delinquency Study and Youth Development Center, Southern Illinois University, 1980.

Kehoe, C. J. Juvenile justice standards: What's in it for the kids and us? *Proceedings of the 110th Congress of American Correctional Association,* 1981, 201-205.

Morris, D. J. A step in the right direction. *Together,* 1980, Winter, 3-5.

Murray, C. *The link between learning disabilities and juvenile delinquency: Current theory and knowledge.* Washington, D. C.: U. S. Government Printing Office, 1976.

Norde, G. A survey among correctional educators. *Needed* teacher-education training programs for correctional education. *Offender Rehabilitation,* 1977, *3,* 257-261.

Norman, S. *Detention practice.* New York: National Probation and Parole Assn., 1960.

Prout, H. T. The incidence of suspected exceptional educational needs among youth in juvenile correctional facilities. *Journal of Correctional Education,* 1981, *32,* 22-24.

Roush, D. An educational survey of administrative, program, and supervisory personnel in Michigan detention facilities. *Counterpoint,* 1981, Summer, 27-35.

Roush, D., & Morris, D. J. Issues in detention education. *Proceedings Journal of the Michigan Association of Teachers of Emotionally Disturbed Children,* 1980, *1,* 1-4.

Roush, D., & Steelman, B. T. A team approach to detention staff development. *Juvenile & Family Court Journal,* 1981, November, 33-43.

Smith, H., Wydra, D., & Klotz, L. Interagency cooperation in serving the exceptional child in Louisiana's correctional facilities. *Journal of Correctional Education,* 1981, *32,* 14-16.

Wolford, B. Education: An effective bridge between the correctional institution and the community. *Journal of Correctional Education,* 1980, *31,* 15-16.

The Realization of Potential by Lorton, D.C. Inmates with UDC College Education Compared to Those without UDC Education

Gilda Moss Haber

Introduction

This is a study of 118 residents of a Medium Facility Correctional Institution at Lorton, Virginia. While the facility is in Virginia it is a part of, and is administered by, the D.C. Department of Corrections. We will simply refer to this facility henceforth as "Lorton."

The 118 residents of this study were divided into two groups. The first group composed of 56 residents was enrolled in a university college program at Lorton administered by the University of the District of Columbia. The second group of 62 residents was composed of men at Lorton who were *not* in the college program. We will refer to those in the college program as the "college" group and those not in the program as "the non-college group." All 118 of the respondents were black males from economically and culturally deprived inner city Washington, D.C.

The purpose of this study was to identify the differences, if any, between residents of Lorton in the college and in the non-college groups. Ultimately we should be able to predict who will or will not fit in well with the college program and if the college group as we suspect, has less recidivism after release from Lorton, than the non-college group, we would then be able to predict and thereby to some degree, control recidivism among residents.

The college and non-college groups are examined in a three phase study. Phase I dealt with the background of the two groups, college

Gilda Moss Haber, PhD, is with the Department of Criminal Justice, University of the District of Columbia, Van Ness Campus, 4200 Connecticut Avenue, NW, Washington, D.C. 20008.

and non-college, while incarcerated at Lorton. The two groups were studied as to their characteristics on five variables. These five variables were:

1. Family Background,
2. Education of the Respondent and Family,
3. Program Evaluation,
4. Sentence Structure,
5. Sociometric Data.

The author reported the differences between these two groups on the five variables in an earlier paper and will summarize them shortly. A sixth variable, a measurement of realization of potential, the Personal Orientation Inventory (POI) (Shostrom, 1968), was also used to measure and compare mental health of the two groups and to compare scores. It is a comparison of the scores of the two groups on the POI which is the object of this paper. With the sixth variable having been analyzed, Phase I of the research will have been completed.

Phase II will study the differences between Lorten, D.C. black males and Lorten, D.C. *ex*-offenders. Again, approximately half of the sample will be enrolled in the UDC college program and about half will not have been enrolled in the college program while at Lorton. The object of this phase will be to study the adjustment of the college and non-college group to society, looking again at some of the earlier variables such as family (adjustment rather than background), at educational progress or usage, at work relations, at sociometric relations among peers and family, and of course, at recidivism. We plan to test the hypothesis that those formerly (or still) enrolled in the UDC college program will adjust better to society and will have a significantly lower rate of recidivism than those ex-offenders who have not been enrolled in the college program while at Lorton.

Phase III of the study will examine black males of inner city D.C., from the same deprived background as the Lorton and ex-Lorton groups, who have never been incarcerated. As in Phases I and II there will be two groups, one with college a education and one without. These groups will be examined to find why, when apparently coming from the same socioeconomic and culturally deprived background as the Lorton residents, these men did *not* become offenders.

Thus this study includes both applied and basic research. The applied research is to be a measure of the impact of college education on offenders, ex-offenders, and the never-incarcerated. Is a college program for offenders cost-effective? We think it is, but we must document this with supporting evidence. The basic research involved relates to the question as to why and how some men, apparently coming from the same background, do and others do *not* become offenders. How, why, and when does college education help or attract certain types of offenders and non-offenders? What does it do for ex-offenders?

The hypothesis beneath all of these studies is, of course, that there is a difference among those men who participate in a college program and those who do not. We expect to find that those in Lorton are significantly different when enrolled in the UDC college program from those not enrolled. We expect to find among the differences, better adjustment while at Lorton and after release, and a lower recidivist rate among ex-offenders who were enrolled in the college program compared to those who were not enrolled in the college program.

We have found no published study addressed to the differences among offenders who have received college education and those who have not. However, at a recent national meeting of the Academy of Criminal Justice Sciences, we had occasion to listen to several papers on college education in prisons. The papers presented by Auffrey (1983), Fortune (1983), Lofgreen (1983), and Reed (1983) examined rehabilitative effectiveness of education, learning styles of the incarcerated versus the on-campus college student, the relationship between education and employment of selected offenders from a state prison, and the motivation of inmates for college enrollment, respectively. Wolford (1983) conducted a survey of post-secondary institutions providing educational programs for the incarcerated.

The research presented in the author's earlier paper and in this paper differs from those presented at the Academy of Criminal Justice Sciences' meeting in the following respects:

1. This research used a larger sample (N = 118) than others.
2. Our sample was a random stratified sample unlike those of the other studies.
3. Our research used a control and experimental group, thereby using comparative groups.

4. Our research identifies the characteristics of the two groups.
5. In our study statistical measurements were used.
6. The use of a standardized personality test (POI).
7. We specifically studied those enrolled in a *college* program whereas other studies lumped all educational and vocational programs together and "evaluated" them.
8. This study dealt with black males only, which make up the largest single incarcerated group.
9. This study dealt with and will continue to deal with men all coming from the same socioeconomic background.
10. This study includes applied and basic research.

Each of the studies referred to previously lacked one or more of these characteristics. Wolford's, however, should not be included in a comparison of this study since it was simply a survey of educational opportunities available to the incarcerated, unlike all of the other studies which were empirical.

Before discussing our findings on the differences in mental health found on the Personal Orientation Inventory between the college and non-college groups at Lorton, we will briefly describe the method by which our data was collected and present the findings of the first paper comparing the background of the two groups.

METHOD

Sample

Each of the 56 men of the college group at Lorton was selected by a random stratified sample from the list of the 250 men enrolled in the college program (out of a total of 1200). The 68 men in the non-college group were likewise selected by a random stratified sample from all of the remaining 950 men not in the college program. The time of this phase of the study was in the Spring of 1982.

Instruments

Two measuring instruments were used for the data collected. The first was an in-depth questionnaire with over 100 questions, asking about the five variables mentioned earlier, family background, education, program evaluation, sentence structure, and sociometric data. The questionnaire was administered through an interviewer who asked each question and filled in the respondent's answers.

The second measure was, as indicated earlier a standardized test with some 13 measures of personality. The test consisted of over a hundred statements, each with two possible answers. Respondents had to select which of the two answers best represented them. The scores of each respondent were added and the mean score on each measurement compared with the mean scores obtained for other non-incarcerated and incarcerated groups. We elected to compare the college and non-college group means of our study with the group mean obtained for normal male college students. As the earlier paper discussed findings on the first five variables, this paper will discuss findings on the Personal Orientation Inventory together with those on the background of each group, college and non-college, so as to obtain a composite picture of the two groups.

The Research Team

In order to design, collect, and code the data for this study, the author worked with men at Lorton who were students in two successive Research Methods classes she taught at Lorton. It was felt that residents of Lorton, trained to interview and who had participated in the research from its inception, would make the best interviewers. They were more likely, it was felt, to get responses and mainly truthful responses from other residents, since they themselves were residents. Residents might react with more reserve to questions from "outsiders."

Accordingly the author constructed an interview together with the men in the first (Introductory) Research class and trained these men to interview the respondents listed in the sample. To the best of our knowledge this is the first time that an inmate group has been trained to construct an interview and to actually interview others within a correctional facility. The Research class was also trained to administer the POI. In the second Research Methods (Advanced) class, some men from the first class continued on and some new students enrolled. This class was trained to construct a code in the format desirable for the computer, and then coded all of the responses to the more than 200 questions (including the questionnaire and the POI), for the 118 respondents.

We must mention that the Research Methods classes were among the best classes the author has ever taught. The men were hardworking, responsible, even daring, since they knew it was taking a chance to ask questions—often intimate questions—in what many of them described as a "hostile environment" where "questions were dangerous." One man was given a bloody nose by an irate respondent, yet went on to assume the load of interviews left by one man who was released from the institution and by another who went "behind the wall," i.e., he was put into maximum security for some infringement of the rules. We all had to work within time limits constrained by "counts" and there was virtually no telephone communication between the author and the students. Meetings could only be conducted in the twice weekly classes. The author was very fortunate, however, to have two students who undertook to organize the class during her absence and to keep the flow of interviews and collection of data going. All of the other students, too, worked hard and were extremely reliable, turning in all of the work they had promised. There was only one miscreant; however, this is not unusual in a group of 25 researchers.

The morale of this group was extremely high. Moreover, the author found, in administering the POI test to the research group (which was *not* part of the sample used of college men) that the research team scored higher than the other college men, and higher than some non-incarcerated groups such as Vista Volunteers. The author had given them the POI test and the interviews to fill out one month after the class in research began. They were told that they were filling out the interview and POI tests "for practice" and "to time" these measurement tools. In effect we wanted to see if the research group differed from the other groups as a result of their intensive research experience. We now know that they differed on the Personal Orientation Inventory—they were far superior to the non-incarcerated college group, to the rest of the Lorton college group, and to the non-college Lorton group. Whether they differ on background is the subject of another paper to be presented later this year.

Analysis

We analysed the findings by comparing the responses of the two groups using the Chi Square measure of the differences between the two groups at the .05 or less level of significance. Next, we will present the findings of differences between the two groups based on the five variables mentioned earlier, family, education, program evaluation, sentence structure, and sociometrics. All of the differences between the two groups, as presented below, were significant at the .05 or lower level of significance.

FINDINGS

Family Background

Although all of the respondents came from an economically and culturally deprived family of inner city D.C., the college group was not quite as deprived as the non-college group. The fathers of the college group left the family less often than in the non-college group and when they had left, they left when the respondent was eight or over. In the non-college group the fathers who had left the family had left when the boy was less than eight years old. When the college group's father did leave the home, he helped support the family more often than did fathers of the non-college group. In all of the above differences the $p \leq .05$.

Education and Occupation

In the college group more of the fathers, mothers, and even wives of those married were reported as having some college education, than was the case among the non-college men. The occupations of the fathers of the college group were more often non-manual whereas those of the non-college group were more often manual. More of the college group than the non-college group had been employed immediately before incarceration—considered a good index of post-release employment. None of the college group said they had never worked whereas 17% of the non-college group said they had never worked. This was not due to age since the age range was from 20 to 50 and they had had ample time to work as far as we knew. There might have been a few who had been imprisoned very early and had been incarcerated for a long time, not having had the opportunity to work, but this is more unlikely than likely. Young offenders are not usually given very long term sentences. The differences between the two groups was significant, $p \leq .05$.

Evaluation of Educational Programs

When reasons were given for enrolling in a course of study or training, the college respondents picked constructive reasons such as: "The UDC college education is the best organized program around here," or "It's a way for future improvement," or "It's something I always wanted to do but would never have done on the street. In a way my being here is a blessing." The non-college man was more likely to say such things as "It was the only program available at the time," or "It was something to do." The college group was also considerably more satisfied with its program than were any of the non-college respondents. About 40% of the latter were involved in a variety of programs such as GED and vocational programs. Again, the differences between the two groups was statistically significant.

Sentence Structure

There was a distinct difference in the sentence structure of the two groups regarding their first charge, which is somewhat puzzling. Significantly more of the college group had committed a violent offense such as armed robbery or homicide than the non-college group. However, this was usually their first and only incarceration for the college group. The non-college group on the other hand, had more often committed less serious offenses on their first charge, but had been incarcerated more often, anywhere from two to eight times and could be typified as repeaters, or career criminals. Further, the families of the college group were almost never reported as having been incarcerated. Where members of college respondents had been incarcerated, it was only brothers, but no other relatives. However, it was common for the families of the non-college group to have been incarcerated and it was not only brothers, but all different kinds of relatives who had been incarcerated, fathers, cousins, uncles, nephews, and in-laws. Thus, the non-college group might be considered to have come from a "criminal family" background where experience with incarceration was common and widespread in the family.

When asked if they expected to return to Lorton, 73% of the college respondents said no, but only 53% of the non-college respondents said no. All of the above differences between the groups were statistically significant at the .05 level or less, using Chi Square as a measure of significance.

Sociometric Measures

The college group had few contacts or friends, if any, on the street or if they did, such friends did not visit them at Lorton. The non-college group on the other hand had many visits from street friends while at Lorton. Nor did the families of the college respondents visit them nearly as often as those of the non-college group. Possibly the college men had never had friends on the street in the first place. However, the college group said they got along with the men in their dormitory significantly more often than the non-college group said they did.

These findings suggest that the college group either never had strong ties with street friends or with family, or that they were consciously trying to break off from such relationships. Possibly street people and college men's families were trying to break off with *them.* Perhaps having gone to college, these men no longer fitted in with their former friends and relatives. (The author can remember such a rift at the time that she and a best friend parted ways when the author went on to college and the friend went to work. The non-college friend in this case broke up the friendship.)

One college man in one of the author's classes said, "I don't want to be mixed up with those people on the street. I stay as far away from them as I can." Moreover the college group had more friends at Lorton than the non-college group. The maintenance of ties with deviant members of the street may explain partially why so many of the non-college men are repeaters and so few of the college men are repeaters. This statement is based on conversations with the college administrators at Lorton. The statement is in the nature of a hypothesis at the moment, and will be tested as such in Phase II of the research, due to start in the Summer of 1983.

THE PERSONAL ORIENTATION INVENTORY

We come now to the object of this present paper, a discussion of the difference in scores between the college and non-college groups on the Personal Orientation Inventory—POI. (We shall refer to this test henceforth as the POI.)

As described earlier, the POI is a list of 150 questions of which each of the respondents selects one of two possible answers. The manual on usage of the POI also includes mean scores for various groups which have been tested on the POI. We could have compared the mean scores obtained for college and non-college men at Lorton with those of various other groups such as delinquents, alcoholics, schizophrenics, or with healthy, normal groups (one supposes) such as Peace Corps Volunteers, the management in an electronics company or with normal college males. We opted to use this last group's mean score as a basis for comparison with our own groups, since this was a more rigorous test of the level of performance of those in the Lorton college program and those not in it. A non-incarcerated male college group was, too, the nearest comparative group we could find to the Lorton college group if not to the non-college Lorton group.

The following represents the list of thirteen tests included in the POI and what each of these tests mean. After explaining the meaning of these tests, we will present scores obtained for the college/non-college groups at Lorton, and for the non-incarcerated college males.

T_I— Time Competence Test. This test measures the degree to which the respondent answering the test, uses time competently, i.e., not dwelling too much on the past or future but in being realistically time oriented.

T_I/T_c— This test measures the amount of time that one spends *incompetently* out of larger unit of time. For instance a score of 1.2 means that the respondent spends one hour out of every 1.2 hours incompetently. A score of 5.00 hours means that the respondents spends only one of every *five* hours incompetently. Obviously the first score represents a much less competent respondent than the second instance.

I— This test measures the degree of confidence one has in one's own judgment.

Sav— Strength in one's individual values.

Ex— This test measures flexibility regarding one's own life values and good judgement.

Fr— Fr measures sensitivity to one's own needs.

S— The S measure shows one's degree of spontaneity, the ability to express feelings in spontaneous action.

Sr— Self-regard. This test measures the ability to like oneself and one's degree of feelings of self-worth.

Sa— Self-perception. This test measures one's ability to like oneself in spite of one's weaknesses.

Nc— Measures one's ability to see man as essentially good, and the ability to resolve dichotomies such as good-evil, masculine-feminine, selfish-unselfish, and so on.

Sy— The ability in life to synchronize apparent opposites in life and to relate them meaningfully and compatibly.

A— Measures awareness.

C— Capacity for intimacy.

We hypothesized that the non-college group at Lorton would score lower on all tests than the college group at Lorton. We also hypothesized that the college group would score lower or equally to the non-incarcerated male college group's mean scores.

The following table represents the mean scores on each test in the POI for the non-college and college groups at Lorton and as compared to the non-incarcerated male college scores on each test. In each case the figures reported for each category represents the mean score for the test from each of the three groups, Lorton college, Lorton non-college and the non-incarcerated college male. To the right of each mean score for the Lorton college and non-college groups, we have reported how many score points above or below these scores are, from the non-incarcerated male college scores. At the bottom of the scores of the Lorton college and non-college groups we have added the total number of points each group has scored in *excess* of the scores of the non-incarcerated college males.

It should be noted here that the POI is *not* a measure of education or intelligence, but a measure of the realization of one's potential, of the ability to use one's abilities to the maximum. Therefore, those less educated should theoretically have the same possibility of scoring well on the POI as those with more education. It can be seen immediately that this was not the case. There is a considerable difference in the POI scores of the non-college and college men at Lorton, favorable to the college group. There are several observations to be made.

The first is that the non-college Lorton group scores 6.1 points more than the college group on some scores, and *minus* 11.5 on all others. The Lorton college group, on the other hand scores 16.7 extra score points, more than three times as many points as the non-college group at Lorton, and has only minus .2 points regarding one test.

Table 1

Mean Scores on POI Tests for Lorton non-College and College Groups
Compared with Non-Incarcerated College Males' Mean Scores

			Lorton $\bar{X}$ (Mean)				Non-incarcerated $\bar{X}$ (Mean)
			Non-College		College		College Males
i.	T_1	- Time Competence	13.4	-1.7	15.1	=	15.1
ii.	T_1/T_c	- Ratio of Time Competence	1.2	-3.9	5.3	+0.2	5.1
iii.	I-	- Inner Directed-Confidence in own Judgement	72.5	-3.1	81.0	+5.4	75.6
iv.	SAV	- Strength in Individual Values	17.6	-1.2	19.1	+0.3	18.8
v.	Ex	- Flexibility	16.4	+0.3	18.0	+1.9	16.1
vi.	Fr	- Sensitivity to Own Needs	14.7	+0.9	14.9	+1.1	13.8
vii.	S	- Spontaneous Action	11.4	+1.7	12.2	+2.5	9.7
Viii.	Sr	- Self-Regard	11.5	=	12.7	+1.2	11.5
ix.	Sa	- Self-Perception Liking Oneself	15.0	+1.3	15.3	+1.6	13.7
x.	Nc	- "Man is Essentially Good."	10.4	-1.2	11.4	-0.2	11.6
xi.	Sy	- Ability to Syncronize Opposites i.e. Good-Evil	5.9	-0.4	6.3	=	6.3
xii.	A	- Awareness and Acceptance of own Anger	15.4	+0.3	15.7	+0.6	15.1
xiii.	C	- Capacity for Intimacy	17.2	+1.6	17.9	+2.3	15.6
		Total Additional Points		6.1		16.7	
				-11.5		- 0.2	

Secondly, while the range of extra points for the non-college group is from 0.3 to 1.7, a range of 1.4, the range of the extra points in the Lorton college group is 0.2 to 5.4, with a range of 5.2. Thus the college group has a wider range of scores, almost five times the range of the non-college group at Lorton.

Lastly, the non-college group's scores are lower than the non-incarcerated college males' mean scores on five items equal on one, and higher on six items. Only 46% of their scores are higher than those of the normal college males. The college group at Lorton however, scores lower than the normal college males on only one of the measures and higher on nearly 80% of the tests. The difference is statistically significant when measuring the difference with Chi Square, using the .05 or less measure of significance. This shows clearly that the Lorton college group scored significantly higher than the non-college group, and in half the tests, even higher than the non-incarcerated college group. We may then safely state that the Lorton college group is strongly realizing its potential and that it has a strong degree of mental health. We make this statement with some reservations (yet to be discussed).

Let us look at the strong and weak areas of mental health i.e., maximizing one's potential, in the non-college and college groups at Lorton.

The non-college group scored lower than the non-incarcerated college males on the measures of time competence, confidence in their own judgment, valuing their own potential, feeling that man is basically good and the ability to synthesize apparent opposites such as good-evil, male-female, and so on. In other words the non-UDC college man at Lorton did not use his time fruitfully compared to the college man, lacked confidence in own judgments, had a low valuation of his own potential, showed low level of trust in men, and could not cope with apparent dichotomies such as good-evil, spiritual, carnal, and so on. All of these scores suggest an insecure respondent with a low self-image.

Table 2

Scores of Lorton Resident-College and Non-College groups on the POI which are Lower, Equal or Higher to those of

Non-Incarcerated College Males

	Lower Mean Scores		Equal or Higher Mean Scores		Total	
Lorton Samples	#	%	#	%	#	%
Non-College	6	54	7	46	13	100
College Group	1	8	12	92	13	100
	7		19		26	

$X^2 = 5.0,\ p < .01\ (df = 1)$

On the other hand the high scores of the non-college man suggested that he is flexible, sensitive to his own needs, acts spontaneously, accepts himself together with his weaknesses, accepts his own aggressiveness and anger as natural, and has the capacity for intimate relations.

Let us recapitulate the characteristics of the non-college resident at Lorton as described in the beginning of this paper. He comes from a family that is seriously deprived, both economically and culturally; that has a low level of education and income. He tends to commit non-violent acts but commits crimes repeatedly. His peer group is composed largely of other deviants among family and friends. Add these characteristics to his mental health scores, and then let us reinterpret his mental health scores. We then get the following picture.

The non-college male at Lorton comes from a deprived family background and from a family and peers who operate within a "crime culture." He is a career criminal with repeated offenses and incarcerations. This may be *because* of his personality. He scored high, for instance, on "sensitivity to his own needs." Could this be translated as having to gratify himself at the expense of others? He scored well on "acting spontaneously." Could this be interpreted as acting without thinking of the consequences of the action? He scored highly on "accepting his own anger and aggressiveness as natural." Could this mean he sees nothing wrong with his anti-social behavior? These traits might be good among normal college males, indicating a healthy self-assertion. When described as characteristics of the deviant they may be present in amounts more than healthy, and operating to the detriment of society. Put together with his low scores, we see the non-college man at Lorton as possibly one from a deprived and criminal culture, who satisfies his own needs regardless of who this injures. He is also insecure, he does not trust his own value or judgment and does not trust other people. He cannot synthesize contradictions. He is not maximizing his potential. If we were to grade him on mental health, we might give him a "C."

Now let us look at the Lorton resident enrolled in the UDC college program at Lorton. The Lorton college man only scores *less* than the non-incarcerated college male in regard to the attitude, "Man is basically good." Here he scores very slightly below, 11.4 compared to 11.6 which is the score of the non-incarcerated college male.

The college group at Lorton scores highly on all of those characteristics we noted that the non-college group at Lorton scored well on. He too, even more so than the non-college group at Lorton, is sensitive to his own needs, acts spontaneously, likes himself in spite of his weaknesses, accepts his own aggressiveness and anger as natural and has a strong capacity for intimacy. We thus see that should we be correct in interpreting these characteristics as possibly criminal characteristics when indulged in too much, we might have an explanation for the tendency of the college Lorton group to be more violent albeit only once (so far) than the non-college group. A further point is that both the non-college and the college group showed high tolerance for intimacy. Suppose we see violence against the person as a form of intimacy. Would this then explain the greater number of crimes against the person, the greater amount of violence, seen in the college group? In normal life we have seen the individual who can only achieve intimacy through quarelling or fighting with someone else. Is this a trait of the men at Lorton? On the other hand the high score on intimacy shown by the college group at Lorton might also explain, without being contradictory, the high level of success and enjoyment they had in interviewing other residents. This may also explain the fact that a large number of the author's students in the college program at Lorton, said they would like to work at counseling when they left Lorton. Is this not also an occupation requiring extreme intimacy between the counselor and counselee? In other words, if these men do have these traits, can they be channeled into occupations which are not anti-social and where they will be well-used?

While the college men shared in having a high score on these characteristics just described, they had strengths in another of the tests which are not perceived by the author as possibly anti-social. The college man scored highly on using time competently, being inner directed, or having confidence in his own judgments, he valued his own potential, was flexible and able to synthesize apparent contradictions in life. On two measures he scored far higher, not only than the non-college group at Lorton, but higher than the non-incarcerated college males. These two measures were those of inner-directedness—confidence in one's own judgment—and capacity for intimacy.

We have observed that the college man appears to be more violent and aggressive. However, this very aggressiveness might account for the fact that, unlike the non-college group, he began a program such as the Lorton college program, and stuck with it, unlike the non-college group at Lorton, which frequently had begun programs but dropped out. We certainly feel that this aggressiveness was helpful in locating the residents to be interviewed, and in sticking to the task which was to come back to the Research Methods class with all of the assigned interviews and POI tests completed. Perhaps the Research Team did so well because they had this mix of aggressiveness or drive, and the capacity for intimacy necessary for carrying out a sustained (two hour) period of interviewing with a generally hostile group of people.

The composite picture of the college men at Lorton is as follows. He does come from inner-city Washington D.C., from an economically and culturally deprived area like the non-college group, however, he is at an advantage over the non-college group.

His family is a cut above those of the non-college group in education, income, occupation and in having had a male role figure in the house and or supporting the family, more often and for a longer period than was the case for the non-college man at Lorton. The college man at Lorton is, by definition, more educated, but this was his own choice, and his own accomplishment. Many of the college men at Lorton came there without a high school diploma but entered the education program at Lorton and went on to college at Lorton. However, the college man at Lorton tends to have been violent but is a one time offender. He tends to serve a shorter sentence than the non-college men, so there must be mitigating factors to his offense. The college man at Lorton has *few* associations with deviant street groups, and has few deviant members in his family. As we have seen he scores highly on the POI test often higher than the non-incarcerated college male. He maximizes his potential. If we were to give him a grade on mental health we might give him an "A-." The minus is because he shows a slight amount of distrust for people, and because he has, in the past, realized his potential "natural" aggressiveness often by attacking people. We would hope that, since he has usually applied himself hard to the college program, and tends to dissasociate himself from deviant groups, he will be able to re-channel his aggression into education and or into occupations such as counseling or interviewing which stress organization and intimacy. However, if we were to grade the college man on the basis of realization of potential *at the moment* when this research was carried out, we would give the college man in the UDC program at Lorton the "A-" we suggested earlier. He may have reached his peak potential—for those who participated in the Research Methods classes at Lorton—at the time when he was preparing to, or actually interviewing other residents as part of the research project carried out at Lorton. However, there are other dynamics no doubt operating here, which might explain why the college *Research Team* scored higher than the other college men at Lorton. We shall examine this phenomenon and explain it in a future paper.

We have not yet answered the implicit question, is the high profile of the college man one he came *into* the college program with, or a *result* of his being in the college program? Especially since the Research Team had higher POI scores than the rest of the college men at Lorton, and since the latter had higher POI's than non-college men at Lorton, it suggests that the more intensive their involvement in the college program, or in certain *types* of college experience such as team-work and or interviewing, the higher we can expect their POI or level of mental health to be.

We are planning next to test the POI scores of men at different levels of college education at Lorton, those with none, one, two, three, or four years of college education. We will also test the hypothesis that those in majors emphasizing personal relations with people might score higher than those in less "social" sciences. We might find that the social sciences can best channel the apparent leanings toward both aggression and personal intimacy. Counseling and social work might possibly be the best avenues for these traits. At any rate we may find an explanation, if indeed we do find less recidivism among residents who have been through the college program, of the reasons for less recidivism among them. It may *not* be due to education *alone*. We may find that those who have received more education involving personal relations to have a lower rate of recidivism than others.

Besides testing POI scores at different levels of education, we plan next to implement Phases II and III, beginning in the Summer of 1983 at the latest. This will involve comparing ex-offenders from Lorton who have had some college education with those who have not had any college education. It will also include two such comparative groups from inner city D.C. black males who have never been incarcerated to try to find why, coming from the same groups, apparently, as the Lorton residents and ex-offenders, such men have never been incarcerated. We want to examine successful, as well as non-successful groups from deprived backgrounds. Where did they go *right?*

Meanwhile we have clearly identified two distinct groups at Lorton. One is aggressive to the point of violence but maximizes its potential. The other is less violent but deviant more often. This latter group has a low self-image, is insecure, and minimizes its potential.

If we find, as we expect, that the college ex-offender from the Lorton UDC program is less often a recidivist than is the non-college offender, we will have identified the type of man most likely to succeed while at Lorton and after release. We should then screen out those men as soon as they enter Lorton, by testing them on the interviews and POI's which we have used in this study. However, high scores on the POI might only come after one or two years in the college program.

In the meantime we can use every means at our disposal to encourage candidates with the background characteristics found among the college men in this study, such as those with a less deprived family background, a better work history, first time offenders on a violent charge, and those with weak ties to the deviant culture of the street or in their families, to participate in the college program. If they do not have a high school diploma it does not matter, as we have seen that many men in the college program did not have one either when they entered the institution. What matters is a will to learn and to positively channel aggression. If we do succeed in making this group of men (which represents approximately 10% of the Lorton population) non-recidivists, then we have saved approximately 10% of the entire prison budget for the Washington, D.C. area. This amount of money is no doubt between several hundred thousand and a million dollars. The output for college programs is minute. Thus an aggressive program to include all those suitable for college education would certainly be cost effective. Screening such candidates could become refined. We will no doubt, in the course of this research, develop a standardized way of testing new inmtes, besides interviewing them with the interview already used, to identify those who could benefit from the college program. If we find that this group also has a low recidivist rate, we have more than justified our rationale for carrying out this study. We will also, in the course of this research, develop an understanding as to why some men with poor backgrounds do *not* become criminals. All of this information can be absorbed into a program for preventing crime, reducing crime, and reducing recidivism—all for the benefit of society.

BIBLIOGRAPHY

Auffrey, J. J., & Vandervelde, M. A. *A longtitudinal study of rehabilitative program effectiveness.* Paper presented at the national meeting of the Academy of Criminal Justice Sciences, San Antonio, Texas, March 1983.

Fortune, E. P. *A comparison of learning styles of incarcerated students and on-campus students enrolled in criminal justice coursework.* Paper presented at the national meeting of the Academy of Criminal Justice Sciences, San Antonio, Texas, March 1983.

Haber, G. M. *An evaluation of the University of the District of Columbia and D.C. Department of Corrections Lorton Prison college program at Lorton Correctional Facility.* Paper presented at the national meeting of the Academy of Criminal Justice Sciences, San Antonio, Texas, March 1983.

Lofgreen, V. C. *A grounded theory approach to the education and employment of selected offenders from a state prison system.* Paper presented at the national meeting of the Academy of Criminal Justice Sciences, San Antonio, Texas, March 1983.

Reed, W. E. *Motivation of inmates for college enrollment.* Paper presented at the national meeting of the Academy of Criminal Justice Sciences, San Antonio, Texas, March 1983.

Shostrom, E. L. *The Personal Orientation Inventory.* Edits, San Diego, California 92107.

Wolford, B. I., & Littlefield, J. F. *An examination of post-secondary institutions that provide educational programs for the incarcerated.* Paper presented at the national meeting of the Academy of Criminal Justice Sciences, San Antonio, Texas, March 1983.

Effects of Three Instructional Strategies with Juvenile Delinquents of Differing Learning Styles

Ray B. Hodges
James R. Evans

Research in the neurosciences generally has supported the notion of a direct relationship between certain cognitive skills and patterns of brain function. For example, the left cerebral hemisphere in most right-handed persons has been found to be specialized for verbal/analytic tasks, while the right cerebral hemisphere often appears to be specialized for visual/spatial tasks (Sperry, 1975; McNeil & Hamre, 1974). It is probable that there are individual differences in the relative strength of these cognitive skills, with resulting preferred cognitive modes, or styles, of learning. In the field of education there is evidence that learning is more efficient when students are presented information matched to such individual cognitive or learning skills (Pask & Scott, 1972; Bruininks, 1970).

Galin (1976) reported that the real significance of hemispheric functioning for educators is not that the hemispheres are specialized to work with specific types of materials, but that each hemisphere frequently has a different cognitive style. The left hemisphere-dominant individual's cognitive style should be best suited for analytical, logical modes of instruction which stress auditory and verbal processing of materials for which words are the most appropriate tool. In contrast, right hemisphere-dominant individuals should be more efficient with instructional strategies which stress visual/spatial instructional modes.

Research has indicated that juvenile delinquents usually score higher on performance type intelligence test items that stress visual/spatial learning skills than on verbal type items which stress verbal/

Ray B. Hodges is with the Sullivans Island Public Schools system, Sullivans Islands, SC 29482. James R. Evans is at the University of South Carolina, Columbia, SC 29208.

analytic learning skills (Glueck & Glueck, 1959; Wechsler, 1974; Jerse, 1978). Delinquents, therefore, may constitute a school population which experiences special problems with present school curricula which stress verbal/analytic learning at the expense of visual learning. They often may be forced to remain in an academic program with little chance of succeeding because of inability to master a verbally-based curriculum. When they are removed from public schools for being ungovernable, they traditionally are sent to institutional settings. Institutional education programs also usually concentrate on basic skills in reading and math, and developing those verbal/analytic skills at which the delinquent is least adept.

Due to the unique nature of educational programs for institutionalized delinquents, instructional methods need to have maximum impact on the student in the shortest period of time. Student's lengths of stay may be quite short. If they are to experience greater success when they return to community schools, individualized instructional programs need to be developed which will help remove past educational deficits as quickly as possible (Hodges, 1978). Thus, there is an obvious need for research to examine whether determining a delinquent's preferred cognitive mode and instructing to it can facilitate academic achievement. The present study was designed to do this using the cognitive modes of verbal/analytic and visual/spatial.

It was hypothesized that verbal/analytically competent delinquents would learn better with verbally oriented instruction, while those competent in visual/spatial skills would learn better under an instructional strategy utilizing a visual/spatial type presentation. Furthermore, it was expected that the groups would perform equally well under an instructional strategy combining verbal and spatial approaches.

The Wechsler Intelligence Scale for Children Revised (WISC-R) may offer the educator a viable instrument with which to determine verbal/analytic vs. visual/spatial cognitive style (and, by implication, strength of hemispheric function). Most researchers in the field of neuropsychology, e.g., Lezak (1976), feel that the use of the total Verbal and Performance scaled scores on the WISC-R is not a valid approach to measuring hemisphere function or cognitive mode, but some feel that other clusterings of scores offer a valid approach. For example, in Bannatyne's (1974) approach the subtest scaled scores used to form a "Spatial" category are Object Assembly, Block Design, and Picture Completion. The Vocabulary, Comprehension, and Similarities subtest scaled scores are combined to form a "Conceptual" of verbal skills group. This approach was used in this study since it appeared to permit an accurate diagnosis of relative strengths of verbal/analytic and visual/spatial skills.

METHOD

Subjects

The subjects (*S*s) were 36 right-handed students incarcerated on campuses of the South Carolina Department of Youth Services (DYS) in Columbia, South Carolina. Since recent Wechsler scores and achievement test scores were available for all DYS students, permanent records were examined to find those meeting the Bannatyne grouping criteria. Thirty-six students were selected who met the criteria and agreed to participate.

Twelve *S*s were classified as verbal/analytic, and 24 as visual/spatial learners by Bannatyne's (1974) approach. More specifically, the verbal/analytic learners met the following criteria: (1) combined scaled scores on Bannatyne's "Conceptual" grouping six or more points greater than combined scaled scores on the "Spatial" grouping; (2) a "Conceptual" grouping score equal to or greater than 27; (3) a Verbal quotient on the WISC-R equal to or greater than 90, and a Performance quotient of not less than 70. Visual/spatial learners met the following criteria: (1) combined scaled scores on Bannatyne's "Spatial" grouping six or more points greater than combined "Conceptual" grouping; (2) a "Spatial" grouping score equal to or greater than 27; (3) a Performance quotient on the WISC-R equal to or greater than 90 and a Verbal quotient of not less than 70.

In order to insure that treatment group (class) sizes would be similar to usual DYS classroom student-teacher ratios, the 36 *S*s were divided into three sections of 12 each (i.e., 4 verbal/analytic and 8 visual/spatial learners in each). Scores of only 24 of the 36 were used in the final data analysis in order to match the sections on other critical variables in addition to Bannatyne's grouping. Specifically, it was necessary to use only 12 of the 24 visual/spatial learners, i.e., those who matched the twelve verbal/analytic learners. Within each section the verbal/analytic and visual/spatial learner sub-groups were equated so that the mean age of each was within ±

.5 years, and the mean reading grade placement level of each, as measured by the Wide Range Achievement Test, was within ± .5 years. Additionally, each sub-group's mean full scale IQ was within ± 2 points of the other. There also were four subjects from each of the three geographic regions of South Carolina in each section to help minimize the effects of familiarity with specific instructional content. It was impossible to match the sub-groups on sex and race; out of the total population of 340 students, only 12 verbal/analytic learners were found and no black females were among them. Secondly, there were only three black females who met the desired criteria for visual/spatial learner and who agreed to participate in this study. Subject characteristics are summarized in Table 1.

Procedure

An instructional unit was prepared on each of the three geographic regions of South Carolina, i.e., "Up Country," "Low Country," and "Midlands." These units were designed so that each was similar in content type and level of difficulty. Units in geography were chosen because the subject matter of geography easily can be presented through verbal/analytic, visual/spatial, or combined instructional approaches.

After development of the units, each geographic region of the state was assigned a number. Numbers then were drawn at random. The unit for the first area chosen was taught by a verbal/analytic instructional approach, i.e., tapes, lectures, class discussion and written review handouts. The second unit was taught by a visual/spatial instructional approach, i.e., maps, slides, problem solving activities in game form. The third was taught a combined instructional approach, i.e., one which combined the verbal and spatial methods mentioned above. This procedure was designed to insure that the units and methods of instruction were randomly matched.

Each of three sections of twelve subjects received separately five days of instruction in each of the three areas of South Carolina geography. Geographic areas taught (and, hence, instructional strategies used) followed in identical sequence for all three groups, i.e., Up Country by verbal/analytic, Low Country by visual/spatial, and Midlands by a combined approach. This sequence of unit presentation was selected from a book of random numbers. A five day break was provided between each of the five day instructional periods to minimize effects of previous learning sets. Immediately

Table 1

Subject Characteristics

Learner Type	N	Age		Reading Level		WISC-R IQ		Race/Sex	
		$\bar{X}$	S.D.	$\bar{X}$	S.D.	$\bar{X}$	S.D.	Black by Sex	White by Sex
Verbal/Analytic	12	15.0	.8	7.5	1.2	91.2	4.7	6M*	2M, 4F
Visual/Spatial	12	14.8	.7	7.8	1.5	92.8	4.5	2M, 2F	4M, 4F

*M = Male, F = Female

following each instructional period a post-test was administered. To help insure that instructional objectives and post-tests for each unit were equivalent, objectives and post-tests were designed so that identical geographic features of each region were taught and included in test items. The only apparent differences in each unit's objectives and tests were the changing of proper nouns to denote regions. To measure reliability of the post-tests, split half (odd/even) reliability coefficients were computed for each. These ranged from .73 to .76 (corrected for attenuation).

To minimize effects of researcher/subject interaction and to model a normal classroom learning situation, a teacher unaware of the hypotheses of the study or learning styles of the specific students was trained to teach the three units. The teacher was a thirty-five-year old female with ten years of teaching experience in public and institutional school settings. She was certified and experienced in both reading and social studies with regular and special education students. A pilot study was conducted by the researcher to familiarize the teacher with the desired instructional approaches prior to the actual study. Students in the pilot study were not included in the final sample.

RESULTS

Means and standard deviations of the post-test scores are shown in Table 2.

A two groups by three repeated measures analysis of variance (ANOVA) design was used with post-test scores as the criterion variable. The main hypothesis to be tested was that there would be a significant interaction between learner type and instructional strategy, i.e., visual/spatial learners scoring higher under the visual-spatial strategy and verbal/analytic learners scoring higher under the verbal strategy. No group differences were expected with the "combined" instructional strategy.

The learner type by instructional strategy interaction did not reach acceptable levels of significance ($F = .48$, $p = .62$), thus failing to provide support for the main hypothesis. The expectancy that the two learner types would not differ on a combined instructional approach was supported by this lack of a significant interaction. The only significant main effect obtained was for instructional type. A Scheffe's procedure indicated that this was accounted for

Table 2

Means and Standard Deviations of Post-test Scores

Type	N	Verbal Instruction		Visual Instruction		Combined Instruction	
		Mean	SD	Mean	SD	Mean	SD
Verbal/Analytic Learners	12	85.3	10.0	86.8	7.7	80.2	10.0
Visual/Spatial Learners	12	78.0	11.5	87.7	7.9	69.9	22.2
Total	24	81.6	10.7	87.2	7.8	75.0	16.1

primarily by scores based on the combined instructional approach being lower than those following the other instructional strategies; however, inspection of individual scores revealed that the very low score of a single visual/spatial learner was the likely cause of this result.

Further data analyses were made because inspection of group means suggested that these often were in predicted directions. Mean scores of the visual/spatial learners under verbal and visual instructional strategies were compared with a *t*-test procedure. This difference was significant at the .001 level. ($t = 4.343$; 1-tailed test), with the higher scores under the visual strategy. The same type comparison was made between means of the verbal/analytic and visual/spatial learners under the verbal-type instructional strategy. This difference was significant at the .05 level ($t = 1.845$; 1-tailed test) with verbal/analytic learners having the higher scores. To control for overall type I error resulting from these multiple *t*-tests, the Bonferroni procedure was applied. With this procedure only the difference between scores of the visual spatial learners under verbal and visual instructional strategies can be considered significant ($p = .015$).

DISCUSSION

Results were not supportive of the *general* notion that using instructional strategies consistent with preferred learning styles of delinquents facilitates their academic achievement. However, there was support for this in regard to delinquents with relative strength in visual/spatial learning. That learner-type scored significantly higher under visual/spatially oriented instruction than under verbal type instruction. This may be an especially meaningful finding because there is a general consensus that the vast majority of delinquents are more capable in non-verbal skills areas (including visual/spatial skills) than in verbal areas. In fact, in selecting *S*s for this study, it was found that only 3% of the entire DYS population met the criteria of this study for verbal/analytic learner, while there were a great many meeting the visual/spatial criteria.

For those relatively few delinquents who are adequate verbal learners it does not seem to matter how material such as involved in this study is taught. However, for visual/spatially oriented delinquents a visual approach may be much more effective. In this study the latter type *S*s mean scores not only were significantly higher under the visually oriented teaching strategy, but 10 out of 12 of these did better under that strategy than under a verbal strategy.

It is possible that the nature of the material taught precluded an adequate test of the learner type-instructional procedure interaction. Geography subject matter as used here may lend itself so well to a visual approach that even the low visual/spatial aptitude level of the verbal/analytic learners was adequate for mastery of the material when taught in a visual/spatial manner. Another alternative explanation for the findings relates to the scarcity of delinquents with relative strength in verbal/analytic skills. Considering this low incidence and the limited reliability of WISC-R subtest scores, it is possible that some of the "verbal/analytic learners" were inappropriately selected. That is, perhaps the high verbal-low spatial nature of the scores was not a true reflection of their cognitive skills, but a function of the unreliability of the selection process. Future researchers may find it especially fruitful to attempt replication of this work using different subject matter and larger numbers of delinquents classified as verbal/analytic learner.

REFERENCES

Bannatyne, A. Diagnosis: A note on recategorization of the WISC scaled scores. *Journal of Learning Disabilities*, 1974, *7*, 272-273.

Bruininks, R. H. Teaching word recognition to disadvantaged boys. *Journal of Learning Disabilities*, 1970, *3*, (1), 28-37.

Galin, D. Educating both halves of the brain. *Childhood Education*, 1976, *40* (53), 17-20.

Glueck, S., & Glueck, E. *Unraveling juvenile delinquency*. Cambridge, Mass.: Harvard University Press, 1950.

Hodges, R. *An evaluation of the curriculum of Birchwood High School and proposal for alternative curriculum design. May 9, 1979: A report to the superintendent.* Unpublished manuscript, 1979.

Jerse, F. W., & Fakouri, M. W. Juvenile delinquency and academic deficiency. *Contemporary Education*, 1978, *49* (2), 106-109.

Lezak, M. *Neuropsychological assessment*. New York: Oxford University Press, 1976, 122-126.

McNeil, M. R., & Hamre, C. W. A review of lateralized cerebral hemispheric function. *Journal of Learning Disabilities*, 1974, *7* (6), 375-383.

Pask, G., & Scott, B. C. E. Learning strategies and individual competence. *International Journal of Man and Machines*, 1972, *4*, 217-253.

Sperry. R. W. Lateralization in surgically separated hemispheres. In B. Milner (Ed.), *Hemispheric specialization and interaction*. Cambridge, Mass.: MIT Press, 1975.

Wechsler, D. *Wechsler Intelligence Scale for Children-Revised*. New York: The Psychological Corporation, 1974.

The Incidence of Communication Disorders of Male Inmates in the Texas Department of Corrections

Robert L. Marsh

ABSTRACT. The objectives of this study were to determine the incidence of communication disorders in two random samples of male inmates, one group entering and another group exiting the Texas Department of Corrections. The incidence of disorder in the two groups was compared with the normal population to determine if there was a higher occurrence among prisoners. Those exhibiting a disorder were compared on a number of demographic variables.

The study indicated that the incidence of disorder among prisoners was not dramatically higher as the majority of other studies in this area have indicated. Positive correlations were found between age and hearing loss in the exiting group. A negative correlation was found between educational achievement and articulation disorders in the entering sample. The chi square statistic was significant between race and articulation disorders in both samples.

Introduction

An impressive amount of research as well as philosophical discussion has been devoted to the concept of rehabilitation of the offender. During the approximately 200 years since the beginning of the American penal system, the philosophy of confinement has changed from meditation to retribution to a mixture of retribution and resocialization.

The reordering of the American penal system through the last 200

Robert L. Marsh, PhD, is Associate Professor of Criminal Justice, Graduate School of Public Affairs, University of Colorado at Denver, 1100 14th Street, Denver, CO 80202.

years has focused on providing a broader range of services to aid in the treatment and resocialization of the offender. This orientation has led researchers to not only search for more effective treatment methods but also has stimulated the inquiry into the causes of criminal behavior. Although various disciplines have dominated this inquiry at various times in the past, many current researchers are focusing on an eclectic or "systems" approach.

Historically, the maintenance and improvement of the general welfare of the incarcerated has been recognized as an important goal with vocation and educational programs specifically evolving from this concept. In addition, penal systems, on their own volition and as a result of court decisions, provide medical, dental, psychological, recreational, and religious services to inmates in order to improve their welfare. In providing for the welfare of those incarcerated, as well as searching for casual variables of criminal behavior, activities are constantly expanding into areas that were largely unrecognized in the past. A recent developmental area has been an inquiry into the incidence of communication disorders in incarcerated populations. While there is a large amount of data available regarding the normal population, very few studies have been conducted on prison populations. Furthermore, those studies completed indicate a disproportionately high incidence of disorders in inmate groups. The American Speech and Hearing Association (1973) noted that prisoners are "neglected" with few diagnostic and remedial services available to them.

Research on Speech and Hearing Disorders of Adult Inmates

A few early criminologists and penologists (Healy & Bronner, 1926) alluded to the existence of various communication disorders in adult criminal populations. The first study by speech pathologists directed toward adult criminals was made by Charles Van Riper and Bryng Bryngelson in 1934. In this study, the authors reported an abnormally high incidence of speech and hearing disorders.

In 1934, Palmer conducted a study at the Kansas State Penitentiary in Lansing, Kansas, to determine the incidence of speech and hearing disorders. His methodology was not rigorous and principally consisted of personal interviews with prison officials. He reported that the incidence was observed to be roughly twice that of the normal population.

During this early period, even though the number of studies regarding adult criminals was extremely limited, a number of studies on juvenile delinquents was conducted. Slawson (1926) reported, in a study of 1,648 juvenile delinquents, that the delinquent group had a four to ten times higher incidence of hearing impairment.

Molitch and Adams (1936) noted that, based on their study of 360 juvenile delinquents, a positive correlation existed between behavioral problems and hearing disorders.

In 1965, Deck partially replicated Palmer's earlier study at Kansas State Penitentiary. This descriptive study included 1,602 male inmates, approximately 15 percent of whom had speech handicaps. "Disorders of intelligibility accounts for 8.11 percent (N = 130) of the tested population while 3.87 percent (N = 62) had a stuttering handicap . . . "(Deck, 1965:21). The author only found a few significant differences on demographic variables between the speech handicapped and non-speech handicapped groups. The mean IQ of the handicapped groups was 81.16 compared to 88.53 for the non-handicapped group. There was also a larger proportion of blacks than whites with speech disorders.

The audiometric screening test indicated that over half of the subjects had some degree of hearing loss but the majority of the losses were at a single frequency. Among the significant differences noted between the group with hearing losses and the normal group were: (1) a higher mean chronological age for the hearing loss group; (2) a greater proportion of the hearing loss group came from a rural background; and (3) hearing losses were more prevalent among whites than blacks.

Blom (1967) reported in a master's thesis of 1,630 men housed at Indiana State Penitentiary and the Indiana Reformatory that approximately 12 percent of the population indicated some kind of speech disorder. The results of the hearing screening showed that 35 percent of the adults failed while 18.9 percent of the juveniles failed.

Melnick (1970) reported in a study of hearing impairment in 4,858 male inmates in Ohio that 40 percent failed the screening with the majority of the failures in the high frequencies. Of this 40 percent only 2.4 percent of the total sample had a biaural (both ears) hearing problem. The author concluded that the "hearing status of this group is similar to that found in the general population, when age and sex are considered."

Gardner (1975) conducted a hearing screening of 50 randomly selected male inmates at Utah State Prison. He found that 48 percent failed at one or more test frequencies. Of this number, 22 percent had serious hearing losses in the speech frequencies.

The results of an evaluation of 128 men at Patuxent Institution in Maryland was reported in 1972 (Walle, Kandel, Boslow, & Reading, 1972). The sample group was self-referred or referred by the staff. Although the selection process was biased, the results indicated that 50 percent of this group evidenced a significant communication disorder. Thirty-four percent had clinically significant articulation problems, 34.9 percent hearing disabilities, 17.5 percent stuttering problems, 9.5 percent voice problems, and 3.2 percent language disorders.

Since this was not a random sample, the results should be compared with the figures reported by Reading (1973) who later screened and evaluated all of the inmates at Patuxent Institution (N = 522). The incidence of those exhibiting a clinically significant communication disorder was 7 percent, articulation disorder was 4 percent; and voice disorder 6 percent. The average IQ of those with a communication disorder was 80 and of the total group 91.

In two other unpublished reports referred to in the Task Force Report on Speech Pathology and Audiology and Service Needs in Prisons, a high incidence of disorder was reported. James Mack (1973) found that 3 percent of the inmates in the Lebanon, Ohio, Correctional Institution had a pathological speech condition requiring attention and 5 percent had a hearing problem. Curt Hamre (1973) reported in his study of the inmates at the Marquette Correctional facility in Michigan that 23 percent failed the hearing screening and 39 percent evidenced a speech problem.

The wide variability in the incidence of articulation disorders reported in the numerous studies conducted in the United States makes it difficult to determine an accurate percentage. The accepted incidence in the non-prison adult population is 4 percent (ASHA, 1952). The incidence in studies regarding prison populations ranges from 3 percent to 39 percent.

Research into speech and hearing disorders in inmate populations is related to the two theoretical concepts previously discussed. First, the discussion into criminal causation is still a dynamic inquiry. If high numbers of inmates have communication disorders, it would indicate that more intensive research should be initiated to determine the incidence of communication disorders. The focus of this research was primarily related to the second concept.

METHODOLOGY

Selection

Statistically, random samples were taken of male inmates entering and exiting the Texas Department of Corrections to determine the incidence of speech and hearing disorders of an adult inmate population. Ninety-six inmates were selected in the entering group at the Diagnostic Unit. The exiting group consisted of 86 inmates tested at three release points for the system—the Ferguson, Huntsville, and Jester Units. Both groups were given hearing tests to determine the incidence of hearing disorders as well as articulation tests. Demographic data were collected to further describe the characteristics of the two samples.

Audiometric Testing

The audiometric Tests were given with a Beltone Model 12-D, portable audiometer. The hearing screening was divided into two phases. The first phase consisted of a rapid, individual pure-tone screening procedure known as a "pure-tone sweep check." The second phase involved more extensive audiometric screening for those failing the screening in order to determine the extent of hearing disorder.

The screening levels were set at 30dB (International Standardization Organization (ISO), (1964) for the frequencies of 250, 500, 1000, 2000, 4000, 6000, and 8000 Hz. These levels were established on the basis of the American Standards Association (ASA), 1951 levels of 15dB, which have some acceptance as the level of beginning impairment and the adjustment in the ASA 1951 levels required for the International Standardization in 1964. These levels were based on the assumption that losses at the high frequencies did not present a serious problem to speech communication.

From the results of the screening, inmates were classified according to Melnick's model (1970) into one of four categories: (I) passed; (II) failure at two or more frequencies in the same ear at the same test frequencies 4000, 6000, or 8000 Hz; (III) failure at two or more frequencies in the same ear with only one of the failures in the speech frequencies—500, 1000, or 2000 Hz; (IV) failure at two or more speech frequencies in the same ear. Only persons in the fourth category were routinely scheduled for more extensive audiometry.

The degree of hearing impairment in each ear was assigned according to the pure-tone average in the speech frequencies of 500, 1000, and 2000 Hz and were categorized as follows:

Normal	0-26dB
Mild	27-46dB
Moderate	47-60dB
Severe	61-80dB
Deaf	81-higher dB

The type of loss was recorded in one of the three standard classes—sensorineural, conductive, or combined loss.

The second phase of audiometric testing included pure-tone air and bone conduction threshold testing. The Speech Reception Threshold (SRT) was also tested with the Central Institute for the Deaf (CID) Auditory Tests W-1 and W-2. Speech Discrimination scores were obtained with the CID Auditory Test W-22.

The level of ambient noise was measured with an H. H. Scott Sound Pressure Meter, Model 450B on the C Scale. The hearing tests were conducted in the quietest sections of the prison because of the lack of a soundproof testing facility. The settings ranged from unused classrooms to visitation rooms. The noise level varied from 40dB to 60dB in one case. The level was usually constant between 44dB to 48dB. Although some of the noise readings were relatively high, the test personnel were able to hear the tones at 0dB.

Articulation Testing

The general speech testing included two phases. The first part was the administration of the Templin-Darley Screening Test of Articulation (1969). This screening test consists of 50 items that discriminate between normal and deviant articulation. The subject was shown a picture and asked to complete a sentence, initiated by the examiner, regarding the picture's content. If the subject was unable to perform this task, the examiner provided the test word and asked for repetition by the subject.

The majority of the screening tests were administered by a nationally certified, Master's degree level speech pathologist. Assistance was provided by two other state certified, Bachelor's degree level, speech clinicians.

The subject's scores were indicated according to type and severity and results were reported as number of substitutions, omissions and distortions of sounds. Voiced and voiceless "th" errors were disregarded as dialectical differences common to the black groups. The "sh" and "ch" substitutions were disregarded as dialectical differences common to the Mexican-American groups.

The second phase of the speech testing involved evaluation of voice quality. All of the inmates were asked to relate what they saw in two current advertisements in order to obtain a voice sample from spontaneous speech segments. The advertisements contained both pictures and a written narrative. The inmates' responses were tape recorded for one minute. The tapes were evaluated by an American Speech and Hearing Association certified Speech Pathologist. Voice quality was rated according to the following criteria: normal, hypernasal, denasal, breathy, too loud, too soft, inappropriate pitch, and rough. In addition, the taped responses were evaluated for presence of stuttering behavior which was rated on a severity scale of 0 - 7.

The statistics used in this study are descriptive statistics since it had not been established that the incidence of communication disorders in the prison population differed significantly from the normal population. The two statistical tests used were the Pearson product-moment correlation (r) and Chi square.

SAMPLE CHARACTERISTICS

Data were collected on the characteristics of the entering and exiting groups based on age, race, educational achievement, intelligence, recidivism, prior confinements as juveniles, and maximum sentence. Correlations were made to determine if there was any relationship between these variables and hearing loss and articulation errors.

Previous research indicated a positive correlation between speech and hearing disorders and race (Deck, 1965) and IQ (Deck, 1954; Reading, 1973). Because of these earlier reports, it was assumed that persons with lower IQs would score significantly lower in educational achievement tests and have a higher incidence of hearing disorders.

FINDINGS—AUDIOMETRIC SCREENING

Table 1 relates the incidence of hearing disorders in the entering and exiting groups. Class II, III, and IV hearing disorders were higher in the exiting group.

TABLE 1

Incidence of Hearing Disorders

	Entering Group				Exiting Group			
	I	II	III	IV	I	II	III	IV
N =	79	10	4	2	53	15	13	6
% =	83.2	9.5	4.2	2.1	60.9	17.2	14.9	6.9

Age

Table 2 relates the analysis of the entering and exiting groups based on age. Hearing loss is defined by a specific class as noted in the methodology. Class IV failures were the only ones scheduled for more extensive audiometric tests. The table indicated that the majority of the failures were in the exiting group with a wide variability in age. The two failures in the entering groups were older, which was to be expected, since hearing losses increase with age. It is significant to note that three of the six failures in the exiting group were under forty. A Pearson r correlation (.04) for the exiting group was significant ($P < .02$) indicating a positive correlation between hearing loss and age.

Race

Table 3 indicates that there was no correlation between race and hearing loss. Class IV failures were limited to non-black inmates in both sample groups. This differs from previous studies which generally indicated at least equal incidence of disorder between black and white inmates (Deck, 1965).

Educational Achievement

There was no correlation between educational achievement and hearing loss in either sample. The Task Force on Prisons (1973) hypothesized that inmates with significant hearing losses would have lower educational achievement scores. The two failures in the incoming group did exhibit this characteristic with a mean educational achievement score of 1.9 years compared to the overall mean of the

TABLE 2

Class of Hearing Loss by Age in Percentage

Age	Entering Group Class of Hearing I	II	III	IV	Exiting Group Class of Hearing I	II	III	IV
No information	14							
17-30	63	50	50		72	73	38	33
31-40	14	30	50		11	13	8	17
41-50	5			100	8	13	46	17
51-60	4	20			9		8	33
61-70								
Totals	100(79)*	100(10)	100(4)	100(2)	100(53)	99(15)	100(13)	100(6)
	r = .04, DF = 93, N.S.				r = .25, DF = 85, P<.02			

* N's on which above %'s are based.

Note: Total percentages may be less than 100 because of rounding.

TABLE 3

Summary of Statistical Tests for Hearing

Variables	Entering	Exiting
Age	r = .04, N.S.	r = .25, P<.02
E.A.	r = -.10, N.S.	r = -.03, N.S.
IQ	r = -.19, N.S.	r = -.07, N.S.
Prior Prison Confinements	r = .07, N.S.	r = .162, N.S.
Prior Juvenile Confinements	r = -.06, N.S.	r = -.001, N.S.
Maximum Term	r = -.08, N.S.	r = .06, N.S.
Solitary Confinement		r = .18, N.S.

incoming group of 6.4 years. The higher educational achievement level of the exiting Class IV failures (7.6 years) is contradictory to prior findings.

Intelligence

The comparative analysis in Table 3 contributes little to understanding the difference between groups because of the high number (sixty) of exiting inmates with no available test score. Of the eight Class IV hearing failures in both groups, five have no scores available. One previous study (Deck, 1965) indicated that the mean IQ of those inmates with communication handicaps was approximately seven points lower.

Recidivism

Approximately 89 percent of each group had not been incarcerated in an adult prison before. This is slightly higher than the yearly rate of approximately 80-85 percent of entering inmates having no prior confinements in penal institutions. Neither Class III nor Class IV failures in the entering group had been previously confined. Fifteen of the nineteen Class III and Class IV failures in the exiting group had not been confined.

The principal reason for looking at this variable was to determine if recidivism rates were higher for inmates with higher disorders. It was assumed that if communication disorders were correlated to criminal behavior that it would be possible that recidivism rates were higher, but the correlations were not significant.

Prior Confinements as Juveniles

The statistics do not indicate that Class IV failures were incarcerated in juvenile detention centers more than other classes. The entering group did indicate a higher incidence of prior incarcerations compared to that of the exiting group. It was hypothesized if communication disorders were related to criminality, prior incarcerations would be higher. The correlation scores were not significant and did not confirm this.

Maximum Sentence

The average length of sentence in the Texas Department of Corrections is approximately five years. Of the total of eight Class IV failures in both groups, only one person had a more lengthy sentence than the mean. It was hypothesized that the Class IV failures would be more likely to have longer sentences if they were previously incarcerated. The data did not indicate a higher incidence of recidivism or maximum sentence length.

Analysis of Class IV Failures

Table 4 shows the results of the more extensive audiometric tests conducted on Class IV failures. Of the two persons in the entering group, one person had a severe sensorineural loss in one ear and was medically deaf in the other. The other person was diagnosed as having a mild sensorineural loss in both ears.

In the exiting group, the first person was diagnosed as having a severe conductive loss in the right ear. The second person had a moderate combined hearing loss in both ears. The third person had a mild combined loss in the left ear. The fourth person was diagnosed as having a severe sensorineural loss in the right ear. The fifth person suffered from a mild sensorineural loss in both ears. The last person had a mild combined loss in the right ear and a moderate sensorineural loss in the other.

TABLE 4
Analysis of Class IV Failures in Entering and Exiting Groups

Group	Speech Reception Threshold		Speech Discrimination	
	Right	Left	Right	Left
Entering (N=2)	68dB	100dB	86%	76%
	35dB	36dB	72%	72%
Exiting (N=6)	75dB	Normal	36%	Normal
	50dB	53dB	96%	92%
	Normal	37dB	Normal	82%
	65dB	Normal	96%	Normal
	25dB	40dB	76%	68%
	37dB	50dB	92%	92%

FINDINGS—ARTICULATION SCREENING

Age

Table 5 indicates that there was no correlation between the total articulation errors and age. In both groups the majority of persons (71.4 percent in the entering and 56.2 percent in the exiting) were under forty years of age. There was a higher percentage of young entering offenders with articulation disorders than exiting offenders. The higher number of older offenders with problems in the exiting group could be explained by a larger number of long term offenders completing their sentence.

In the entering group fifteen persons evidenced substitution errors compared to seven in the exiting group. In the entering group 73.3 percent (N = 11) were under the age of forty while 42.9 percent (N = 3) of the exiting group were under forty. The data indicated that a higher percentage of young inmates are entering the Texas Department of Corrections with substitution errors. The Product Moment correlation was significant (P = < .01) in the exiting group indicating a strong positive relationship between substitution errors and age.

Although the greater percentage of the inmates making distortion and omission errors in the entering and exiting groups were under forty there was not a statistically significant correlation with age.

TABLE 5

Summary of Statistical Tests for Articulation

Variables	Entering	Exiting
Age	r = .07, N.S.	r = .15, N.S.
Race	x^2 = 6.74, P< .05	x^2 = 14.19, P <.001
E. A.	r = -.28, P< .01	r = -.175, N.S.
IQ	r = .06, N.S.	r = .04, N.S.
Prior Prison Confinements	r = .056, N.S.	r = .114, N.S.
Prior Juvenile Confinements	r = .18, N.S.	r = -.08, N.S.
Maximum Term	r = .003, N.S.	r = .04, N.S.
Solitary		r = .144, N.S.

Race

Twenty-eight persons in the entering group and sixteen persons in the exiting group exhibited articulation errors. In the entering group exhibiting errors, 35 percent were Mexican-American, 42.9 percent black, and 32.1 percent white. In the exiting group exhibiting errors 25 percent were Mexican-American, 43.8 percent black, and 31.3 percent white. Minority members in both samples exhibited the majority of errors. The Chi Square test shows a positive correlation in both samples between minority members and articulation disorders. It should be noted that dialectical differences in black inmates were controlled by disregarding voiced and voiceless "th" errors. Dialectical differences in Mexican-American inmates were controlled by disregarding "sh" and "ch" substitutions.

Deck (1965) found that minority members had a higher incidence of speech disorders than the total population. It is feasible to assume that many minority members had fewer remedial services available at an earlier age to help correct articulation problems.

Educational Achievement

Table 5 indicates that there was a significant negative correlation between persons making articulation errors and educational achievement level in the entering group. The data indicate that the achievement scores of inmates are comparable to that of the total prison population. Previous researchers have hypothesized that communication problems were positively correlated with lower academic achievement. This study does not support this contention. In the entering sample a significant ($P < .01$) negative correlation existed. In the exiting sample the correlation was negative but not significant.

The entering group had over twice as many persons making substitution errors than the exiting group. The exiting group did have three persons with more severe problems (three errors) compared to none in the entering group. All of the persons exhibiting errors had an educational achievement score of six years or less. When the mean score of the entering group making substitution errors is compared to the total incoming sample group, the scores are 1.7 years less. The scores of the exiting group making errors compared to the total exiting sample are 2.9 years less. Scores were not available on six inmates in the entering group making errors and one in the exiting group. The Product Moment correlation showed a significant ($P < .001$) negative correlation in relation to substitution errors the entering and exiting group.

Intelligence

In the entering group the IQ scores of all persons making articulation errors was 26.99 points lower than the total income sample. This confirms the findings of Deck (1965) but the statistical tests were not significant in either sample. The range between the IQ scores of those making errors and the total samples is more detectable in this study than in other studies.

The data in this study also indicate that the mean IQ of entering inmates making substitution errors is 30.3 points lower than the total entering sample. In the exiting inmates making substitution errors the mean IQ is 17.8 points lower than the total exiting sample. The statistical test indicated a significant ($P < .01$) negative correlation in the entering group and was not significant in the exiting group.

In this study the IQ range between the total prison sample and those making errors is larger. The data points to the significance that communication disorders have on a person's learning abilities. Since more speech disorders can be remediated, it further indicates the need for better screening and therapy at an earlier age.

Recidivism

It was hypothesized that if articulation errors were in some way related to criminal behavior, those persons making such errors would have a high rate of recidivism. Rather than indicate this, the data in this study show that the recidivism rate is quite comparable to the total sample groups.

Prior Confinement as Juveniles

As in the discussion of the previous variable regarding adult recidivism, it was hypothesized that a greater number of people making articulation errors would have been incarcerated as juveniles if articulation errors were correlated with criminal behavior. The data did not indicate this in the exiting group. In the entering group 25.0 percent of the persons making articulation errors had been confined as juveniles. This is slightly higher than the 22.1 percent of the total entering sample previously confined but the statistical tests were not significant.

Maximum Sentence

Although those making articulation errors in the exiting group received longer sentences than those in the entering group the statistical tests were not significant.

Solitary Confinement

It was hypothesized that an articulation problem might hinder a person's ability to communicate and result in his being placed in solitary for breach of prison regulations. The data indicated that 37.5 percent of the exiting inmates making articulation errors had been in solitary confinement one or more times but it was not statistically significant.

Findings—Deviant Voice Quality

In the entering group two persons, or 2.11 percent, exhibited a voice disorder. Both of these persons were evaluated as having a "rough voice with vocal fry." Neither person had any other articulation or hearing disorder.

In the exiting group there was one person, or 1.15 percent, exhibiting deviant voice quality. The problem was diagnosed as "rough voice with weak intensity." This person evidenced no other hearing or articulation problem.

Findings—Stuttering

The estimated incidence of stuttering in the normal population is seven out of every thousand persons, or .7 percent. No person in the entering group stuttered. In the exiting group one stutterer, or 1.15 percent, was detected. This person made eighteen repetitions in the reading of a short (one and a half minute) advertisement. The problem was diagnosed as mild to moderate stuttering, rated as three on the seven point severity scale. This person had no hearing or articulation problem.

CONCLUSIONS

Hearing

This study was designed to sample the persons entering and exiting the Texas Department of Corrections. No assumptions were made concerning the likenesses between the sample groups. Instead, the study was initiated to describe the extent of speech and hearing disorders in the two inmate groups.

Hearing disorders in the normal population are estimated at less than 3 percent (HEW, 1970). In the entering sample the percentage of those with serious hearing disorders (Class IV failures) was 2.1 percent (N = 2). In the exiting sample it was 6.9 percent (N = 6). If percentages from both samples are considered together, the overall percentage is 4.5 percent. This is approximately one and a half times the national average but the smallness of the sample may have accounted for the larger percentage.

Since hearing acuity declines with age (HEW, 1970), it was assumed that only older inmates would suffer from hearing loss. Although no significant correlation was found in the entering sample between age and class of hearing loss, the exiting sample indicated a positive correlation ($P < .02$).

Educational achievement scores for the incoming sample were lower for those with hearing problems, but the differences were not statistically significant. The exiting sample with disorders exhibited the opposite results, their scores being higher than the total exiting sample. Although the statistical test was not significant, this variable in particular needs additional study. It is logical to assume that hearing disorders would hamper a person's progress in the educational setting, but the studies completed still give no clear evidence to this conclusion.

Previous research (Deck, 1965) indicated a high incidence of hearing disorders among racial minority members. It was assumed that this study would support previous findings, but it did not. One of the two Class IV failures in the entering sample was white and the other Mexican-American. All Class IV failures in the exiting group were white.

The data in this study do not support the hypothesis that persons with hearing disorders have a lower IQ score. In two Class IV failures in the entering sample, one person had an IQ score lower than the total group and for the other person there was no score available.

The two Class IV failures in the exiting group had higher scores than the mean scores of the group, and four had no available score. Reading (1973) and Deck (1965) found a significant difference in the IQ scores of those with disorders, and those without. There was a negative correlation between IQ and hearing disorders, but it was not statistically significant.

Hearing damage is many times the result of industrial noise, a variety of diseases, and many other causes. Many persons suffering from hearing loss have not had damage from birth, so that IQ scores would not be affected. This variable deserves much further study with particular attention devoted to gathering data on such variables as childhood diseases, medical histories, accidents that affected hearing, work history, and industrial noise.

Persons who were Class IV failures were not more likely to be recidivists (either adult or juvenile) than the total prison population. Although the data in this study do not indicate a relationship, this variable should also be studied in more detail.

This study did not indicate the dramatic incidence of hearing disorders as reported by other studies. One feasible explanation for the difference in incidence reported by this study and other studies is the conservative classification of disorder utilized (Melnick, 1970). Other studies reported any missed frequency as an indication of hearing disorder and this methodological difference in particular produced an extremely high incidence in these samples.

The data in this study indicate that the inmates entering the Texas Department of Corrections had a lower incidence of hearing disorder than the normal population, although the exiting sample had a higher incidence. Further study should be made to determine if this pattern will continue in the future. The incidence of hearing disorder in the entering population verifies Melnick's (1970) conclusions that hearing disorders do not occur more frequently in prison populations than the normal population.

The incidence of hearing disorder in the exiting sample is higher than the national incidence. The most plausible explanation for the difference in incidence in the two samples is the change in the type of inmate entering the Texas Department of Corrections promulgated by the new criminal code which took effect in 1974. The total effect of the new code is still not known, but prison officials report on a subjective level that the characteristics of entering inmates have changed.

Future studies should include larger samples in order to detect the incidence of disorders. This study tentatively confirms Melnick's (1970) conclusions that hearing disorders are not disproportionately high in prison populations.

Speech

Articulation errors were made more frequently by persons under the age of forty (71.4 percent in the entering group and 56.3 percent in the exiting). This indicates that a large number of these persons could benefit from remedial training, but the Pearson r was not statistically significant.

Articulation disorders were more evident among minority members even when dialectical differences were controlled, although differences were not statistically significant. The relationship between articulation disorders and race should be studied in future research to determine if a higher incidence exists in minority groups.

A statistically significant relationship exists between educational achievement and articulation disorder in the entering sample ($r = -.28$, $P < .01$). In the exiting sample a negative correlation exists but it was not significant.

The IQ scores of those persons in the entering group making articulation errors were over twenty-six points lower than the total entering sample, but the Pearson r statistic was not significant. In the exiting group making errors, the score was ten points lower. This parallels the findings of both Reading (1973) and Deck (1965), but indicates a wider range between those making errors and the total sample than the previous studies.

Generally, those persons making articulation errors did not have extensive criminal records either as an adult or juvenile. The hypothesis had been advanced that a correlation existed between criminality and communication disorders (Healy & Bronner, 1926; Van Riper & Bryngelson, 1934; Palmer, 1934). Neither the data from this study nor from other studies support this conclusion. Recidivism should be considered in further studies of this nature because it remains as a critical variable in determining the general relationship between communication disorders and criminal behavior patterns.

The national incidence of articulation disorders is estimated at four percent. In the entering sample twenty-eight (29.5%) made articulation errors. In the exiting group sixteen persons (18.4%) made articulation errors. The average percentage of both samples is 24.4 percent, or six times higher than the national average.

Although the national figures are only estimates of the overall incidence, the incidence of articulation disorders in this inmate population is still important. If compared with articulation errors in primary school groups (K-4th grade), where the data is extensive and constantly about 10 percent (HEW, 1970), the prison population is still two and a half times higher.

This study did not indicate the dramatic incidence of communication disorders as reported by other studies. Particularly in the area of hearing disorders, one feasible explanation for the difference in incidence reported by this study and other studies is the conservative classification of disorder utilized (Melnick, 1970). Other studies report any missed frequency as an indication of hearing disorder and this methodological difference, in particular, produced a higher incidence of communication disorders in prison populations.

Future studies should include larger samples in order to detect the incidence of disorders. Previous studies indicated an extremely high incidence. This study is more comparable to Melnick (1970) who did not find a disproportionately high incidence.

REFERENCES

American Speech and Hearing Association on the Midcentury White House Conference. Speech disorders and speech correction. *Journal of Speech and Hearing Disorders, 17* (June 1952): 129-137.

American Speech and Hearing Association. *Task force on speech pathology and audiology service needs in prisons.* Washington, D.C., 1973.

Blom, E. D. *The incidence of speech and hearing disorders among a felon offender group samples in two state penal institutions in the state of Indiana.* Unpublished master's thesis, Ball State University, 1967.

Bryngelson, B., & Van Riper, C. *Communication problems among prisoners.* Unpublished study, University of Minnesota, 1934.

Deck, G. *An investigation of the incidence of speech and hearing handicaps in a state penal institution: A survey.* Unpublished master's thesis, Wichita State University, 1965.

Gardner, D. V. *A survey of hearing impairments among a randomly selected group of male inmates in the Utah State Penitentiary.* Unpublished master's thesis, Brigham Young University, 1972.

Hamre, C. *Report on communication disorders of inmates at the Marquette Correctional Institution.* Unpublished report on correspondence with the ASHA Task Force on Prisons, 1973.

Healy, W., & Bronner, A. *Delinquents and criminals: Their making and unmaking.* New York: Macmillan, 1926.

Mack, J. *Report on communication disorders of inmates at the Lebanon Correctional Facility.* Unpublished report in correspondence with the ASHA Task Force on Prisons, 1973.

Melnick, W. Hearing impairment in an adult penal institution. *Journal of Speech and Hearing Disorders, 35* (May 1970): 173-181.

Molitch, M., & Adams, P. D. Hearing defects in behavior problems. *Journal of Juvenile Research, 20* (1936): 15-19.

Reading, J. M. *Communication disorders in a correctional facility.* Unpublished paper in correspondence with the ASHA Task Force on Prisons, 1973.

Walle, E. L., Kandel, A., Boslow, H. M., & Reading, J. M. The incidence and severity of communication problems in a sociopathic criminal population. *Correctional Psychologist, 5* (Fall 1972): 71-93.

U.S. Department of Health, Education, and Welfare. *Human Communication and Its Disorders: An Overview.* Government Printing Office: Washington, D.C., 1970.

Benefits Derived from Drug Education for Former Abusers and Offenders

Karen L. Senn

ABSTRACT. A study was undertaken to determine the potential of substance abuse education as a component of an aftercare program. A group of former abusers, half of whom had been incarcerated, participated in a university substance abuse education course. Knowledge, attitudes and drug usage were measured prior and subsequent to the course. Similar data were gathered on regular college students. The former abusers/offenders increased their knowledge significantly, became significantly less accepting in some attitudes, and showed non-significant reductions in drug use. No detrimental effects accrued to college students in the same classroom with the former abusers/offenders.

Background of the Problem

In 1978, San Diego State University was asked by Project JOVE (Job Opportunities in Vocational Education) to provide a Certificate Program in Human Services for a group of former drug and alcohol abusers and offenders. The program was named SPAN (Special Program in Alcohol and Narcotics). SPAN staff requested that a substance abuse course be provided as part of the one-year program of study for the certificate.

Given the innovative nature of providing such a course, an evaluation was initiated at the same time. The study was deemed appropriate as it would contribute to the field of drug education for former abusers/offenders, by providing a data base about an approach to aftercare, namely the provision of a university substance

Karen L. Senn, EdD, MPH, is Assistant Professor of the Department of Health Science, San Diego State University, San Diego, CA 92182.

abuse course as part of an aftercare program. It would also provide information to the university and to Project JOVE for future decisions regarding the sponsorship of such programs.

Recent avenues of addiction research provide evidence that the prevention of relapse is a multifaceted and extensive problem. The expectations of successful rehabilitation which accompanied the initiation of treatment programs have been modified as program evaluations failed to substantiate the belief that individuals could be cured of their abuse and addiction (Wittenborn, Smith, & Wittenborn, 1970). In addition, aftercare programs for people discharged from drug and alcohol abuse treatment programs have not been noted for their success in preventing relapse (Smart, 1976; Wepner, 1970; Wittenborn et al., 1970; Wurmser, 1978). Thus, research has begun to focus on the elements of aftercare programs which might contribute to continued abstinence (Brown, 1979; Marlatt, 1978; Pittel, 1977a, 1977b; Stanton, 1979). There is increasing interest to determine how educational programs might better prevent relapse and recidivism (Chaney, O'Leary, & Marlatt, 1978; Hawkins, 1979; Marlatt, 1978; Marlatt & Marques, 1977; Wurmser, 1978).

The purpose of the study therefore focused on providing information relevant to the knowledge of former abusers/offenders concerning the physiological and psychological effects of drugs and alcohol as well as their attitudes towards the use of habit-forming substances. In addition, this study addressed the potential changes in knowledge, attitudes, and drug usage which might occur with exposure to a substance abuse course; and the implications the above have for the university and for agencies providing services to former abusers and offenders.

SIGNIFICANCE

Recently Marlatt and Gordon (1980) have noted that recidivism rates are high among all of the addictions, including smoking, heroin use, alcohol use and food addictions; and that two-thirds of all relapses occur within the first 90 days following treatment. As a general rule, only 25% of those who enter treatment for any addiction stay to complete the program (Ray, 1978). Evaluations of early methadone programs showed 94% success in ending criminal activity of former heroin addicts (Dole, Nyswander, & Warner, 1968). However, as the programs proliferated, the psychological aspects of the programs diminished because of poor funding and success rates diminished also. In their *Ten Year Perspective,* Dole and Nyswander (1976) summarized much of the methadone work to that date and concluded that the projections of 10 years ago were overly optimistic. They stated that the great majority of heroin addicts remained untreated and programs had lost their ability to attract them to treatment. Controlled studies are lacking on the ability of therapeutic communities to prevent relapse. The subjective reports that do exist are not encouraging. A 1972 Ford Foundation report stated that "It would be surprising if careful evaluation showed that more than five percent of those who come in contact with therapeutic communities are enabled to lead a reasonably drug-free socially productive life" (reported in Ray, 1978, p. 334).

According to Hawkins (1979), deviance results when four elements of the social bond to conventional society are inadequate or missing. He argues that the potential for deviance is lessened if the individual: (1) maintains commitments to conventional lines of action and to achieving the rewards offered through them; (2) has developed skills necessary to attain these rewards in acceptable ways; (3) has developed networks of social supports beyond treatment programs to assist in achieving rewards of a straight life and to provide encouragement and reinforcement for involvement in conventional activities; and (4) believes in moral order and law.

Commitment to conventional activities has been shown to preclude deviant behavior, such as delinquency and illicit drug use (Elliot & Ross, 1974; Frease, 1972; Hirschi, 1969; Kelly & Balch, 1971; Sakumoto, 1978). It is Hawkins' opinion that for rehabilitation to be successful, drug abusers/offenders must make commitments to conventional lines of action, which they have not previously done.

Relapse and community reintegration are not exclusively a problem of former abusers. Ex-convicts and former mental patients are similar to former abusers in that they have usually spent some amount of time institutionalized and usually do not arouse society's sympathy toward their efforts to reintegrate. Treatment programs have often focused on the establishment of their clients as drug-free, crime-free, or illness-free individuals, almost as if it were the drug, the crime, or the illness which were the only problems (Wurmser, 1978).

Thus, while a program philosophy may have espoused the hope that the client continue in a drug-free lifestyle and that the client be reintegrated back into the larger community, most programs have not structured their treatment regimens to assist the client in successfully accomplishing these two tasks. Even where some emphasis has been placed on survival skills, efforts to teach those skills in treatment settings have generally failed to generate the desired outcomes after treatment was completed. This has been found to be the case whether those efforts were directed at drug clients in therapeutic communities (Smart, 1976), at formerly institutionalized mental patients (Fairweather, 1978; Test & Stein, 1978), or at people on parole (Prager & Goldberg, 1977).

Community reintegration efforts by ex-convicts parallel the problems encountered by former abusers. It has become increasingly evident that punishment per se does little to rehabilitate an individual and has done little to reduce the high recidivism rate of prior offenders (Hogges & Hogges, 1976). As recognition of the failure of the correctional system grows, a new objective has emerged, namely, the successful reintegration of the ex-offender into the social community from which s/he has been separated (McKee, 1971). Numerous innovations within prisons have been initiated. These range from approaches that focus on changing the individual to various modifications of the prison environment itself (Sultan & Ehmann, 1970). Within-prison programs usually have as one of their goals the facilitation of community reintegration after release. Such programs include peer-counseling, higher education courses, paraprofessional and new careers programs (Griffin & James, 1979). It appears that higher education is being accepted as a part of prison programs and somewhat more slowly acknowledged as a valuable rehabilitative tool (McVey, 1977). College courses have been offered specifically for inmates and ex-offenders to provide them with more marketable job skills. These have generally been called paraprofessional or new careers programs (Mann, 1973). Evaluation of prison programs, however, does not provide evidence of preventing relapse after release, even though the program environment is superior to the environment in regular prisons (Lynn & Nash, 1975).

Semi-release and post-release programs include peer counseling, work release programs, furloughs for limited duration, release of selected inmates for participation in education and training programs and halfway houses (Sulton & Ehmann, 1970). Evaluation of a variety of parole programs has not indicated a great deal of success in preventing recidivism (Adams & McArthur, 1969; Beckett &

Thomas, 1976; Berecochea & Sing, 1972; Kaplan & Meyerowitz, 1969; Katz, 1977; Kramer & Bass, 1969; Kramer, Bass, & Berecochea, 1968; Platt & Labate, 1976).

Given that many offenders also abuse drugs and alcohol, it may be appropriate to offer substance abuse education to offenders as well as former abusers. This study explored the potential benefits of providing substance abuse education to former abusers, many of whom were also former offenders.

A review of the literature and conversations with individuals involved in the field of addiction and relapse (Falanga, 1980; Hawkins, 1980; Marlatt, 1980) uncovered only one program of formal substance abuse education for former abusers, other than the SPAN program in San Diego. The other program was for inmates at San Quentin Prison, California (Schmidt, Burchiel, & Meyers, 1977).

The program at San Quentin Prison was an undergraduate level course in pharmacology for 28 inmates, most of whom "had prior drug and alcohol problems, and many had been hard core narcotic addicts" (Schmidt et al., 1977, p. 175). The emphasis and focus of the course was on the principles of drug action in the central nervous system, the medical applications of the drugs, and their potential for abuse. The course ran for 17 weeks (2 hours a week) and the inmates received two units of credit from the University of California at San Francisco. The evaluation consisted of a pre- and posttest of 60 objective questions given anonymously. In addition, there was a written requirement to describe the effects of 15 drugs. Fourteen inmates actually completed the course. The reported results of the course were that "Scores on the objective questions from the survey examination increased dramatically . . . [with an] increased ability to recognize differences between the several classes of psychoactive drugs and to identify their actions in terms of risk and benefit" (Schmidt et al., 1977).

The provision of substance abuse education to former abusers has some support in the literature. Based on their own research and other studies to date, Marlatt and Gordon (1980) (and Marlatt & Marques, 1977) made seven recommendations to be included in programs for the prevention of relapse:

1. Relapse drills or role-playing high-risk situations, once they have been identified.
2. Reduction of guilt from a slip by recognizing it as resulting from a lack of practice in certain high-risk situations.

3. Identifying high-risk situations and applying problem-solving techniques in coping with the situation.
4. Practice in decision-making skills, including the weighing of positive and negative outcomes prior to behavior.
5. Taking personal time out for self-rewarding or pleasurable activities (i.e., balancing the "shoulds" and "wants" in life), including participation in relaxation programs such as meditation and physical exercise.
6. Education about the actual effects of the drug or substance involved to help offset the tendency to see the "grass as greener" on the other side of the abstinence fence. Information about the long-range effects of excessive drinking or smoking on physical health and well-being may help counter the tendency to think only of initial pleasurable short-term effects.
7. Program an actual drinking experience under supportive conditions to demonstrate that the relapse need not continue past a one-time ingestion of the substance.

Point number 6 was the focus of this study.

METHODOLOGY

The study employed a pretest-posttest design for the study group and for two non-focal groups.

Comparisons between the groups were made utilizing descriptive statistics (means and medians), and non-parametric tests for significant differences (Chi-square, Mann-Whitney U, Wilcoxon).

Three separate instruments were utilized in order to gather the appropriate data. Knowledge levels were measured through the use of a 305-item multiple choice examination which was drawn from the examination which accompanied the text used in the course. Attitudes of participants were assessed through a self-report scale developed by this researcher, and consisted of 18 continua on various issues related to drug and alcohol usage by society. The use of habit-forming substances by the subjects was measured through the uses of a self-report inventory of the type and amount of various substances used by the participants.

The text selected for the course was *Drugs, Society and Human Behavior* by Oakley Ray (1978). All of the material in the book was covered except for the chapter on oral contraceptives. The course content covered the nervous system, psychopharmacology, the history of drug abuse, alcohol, nicotine, caffeine, over-the-counter drugs, tranquilizers, stimulants, depressants, narcotics, hallucinogens, marijuana, and hashish.

The importance of the affective component of drug education for both the non-abuser and former abuser has been established (Blum et al., 1976; Schaps et al., 1978; Swisher, 1974; Swisher & Horon, 1974). Affective techniques were adapted from *Values Clarification* (Simon et al., 1978), and included: Rank Orders, Twenty Things You Love to Do, Life Line, Ideal Days, and Reaction Sheets. In addition, small group discussion was utilized on issues raised by the instructor and by the student groups making presentations in consultation with the instructor.

The course format consisted of the presentation of cognitive material by the instructor, questions and answers on the material, and then discussions in both small and large groups on related issues, values and attitudes.

COMPOSITION OF GROUPS STUDIED

The population for this study consisted of three groups, one group of former abusers and two non-focal groups of regular college students. The population consisted of two classrooms of students enrolled in the Health Science 574 Habit-Forming Substances class during the fall semester 1980 at San Diego State University. One classroom was composed of students who were members of the SPAN program (former abusers/offenders) and a group of regular college students enrolled in the same class (NSPAN). The third group of students was composed of individuals who had chosen to enroll in another HS574 Habit-Forming Substances class which was offered in the evening by the same instructor (NIGHT).

The SPAN group was composed mostly of white males and females between 25 and 34 years old, with half unemployed and half having no more than a high school education. Sixty-four percent had arrest records and 55% had jail records for drug and alcohol related offenses.

The NSPAN group was composed mostly of white females between 20 and 24 years old, mostly employed part-time with a majority having 3 years of college education and no arrest or jail records for drug and alcohol related offenses.

The NIGHT group was composed mostly of white males and females between 20 and 29 years old, mostly employed full-time with a majority having 3 years of college education and no arrest or jail records for drug and alcohol related offenses.

The three groups differed significantly ($p < .05$) on the characteristics of age, education, employment and prior arrest/incarceration. There were no significant differences between the ethnic background and sex composition of the groups.

FINDINGS

Table 1 presents the statistical summary of the pretest and posttest scores for all groups. The mean gain in knowledge was calculated for each group. SPAN showed a mean gain of 100, NSPAN a gain of 97, and NIGHT a gain of 68. The difference between the SPAN and NIGHT means on the pretest was 37, but on the posttest the difference was only 5. Thus the SPAN group gained relative to the NIGHT group. The significant difference that had existed between them on the pretest was no longer evident on the posttest.

An examination of the group means for SPAN and NSPAN shows that the difference in the pretest means (31) was approximately the same as the difference in the posttest means (28). Thus the SPAN group neither gained nor lost ground over the duration of the course when compared with the NSPAN group.

No significant differences emerged at the $p < .05$ level when the attitude data were analyzed as a whole. However, when the continua were divided into subsets some significant differences emerged. The subsets were: attitudes toward former abusers, normative attitudes, and attitudes toward legal, illegal and prescription drugs.

Table 2 presents the median scores for the combined continua in each of the above-mentioned categories, and indicates which changes from pretest to posttest were significant as a result of applying the Wilcoxon test. SPAN showed a significant change only on normative issues toward being less accepting in this area. NSPAN showed significant changes toward less accepting attitudes in three areas, i.e., legal, regulatory and normative issues. NIGHT significantly changed their attitudes toward illegal drugs and became more accepting in this area. All other categories showed non-significant changes but two trends did emerge. SPAN and NSPAN generally changed their attitudes toward the less accepting end of the scale; however,

Table 1

Statistical Summary of Pretest and Posttest Scores for All Groups on Knowledge Exams

Group	N	Mean	SD	Median	Range	Mode	Skewness	Kurtosis	Mean Gain
					Pretest				
SPAN	14	45.7	16	45.5	54	none	-.013	-.686	
NSPAN	16	77.2	21.4	78.5	83	85	-.945	1.328	
NIGHT	17	83	25	83	89	92	-.467	-.206	
					Posttest				
SPAN	14	146	32	132	97	none	.752	-.829	100
NSPAN	16	174	30	160	117	159	.683	.223	97
NIGHT	17	151	12.4	148	39	142 159 167	.242	multi-modal	68

Table 2

Combined Median Scores for Attitude Subsets for All Groups on Pretest and Posttest

	SPAN		NSPAN		NIGHT	
	Pretest	Posttest	Pretest	Posttest	Pretest	Posttest
Legal	4.2	3.8	4.0	2.9*	5.1	4.6
Legal/Prescription	4.5	3.1	3.4	2.6	4.4	5.3
Illegal	3.8	4.0	4.0	3.1	4.3	5.4**
Regulatory Issues	4.2	3.8	3.5	2.3*	4.2	3.7
Normative Issues	4.8	4.2*	4.6	4.0*	5.8	6.5
Former Abuser Issues	3.3	2.7	2.9	2.4	3.0	3.7

*Subset showed significant ($p < .05$) change toward less accepting end of the scale.

**Subset showed significant ($p < .05$) change toward more accepting end of the scale.

SPAN N = 14
NSPAN N = 13
NIGHT N = 13

NIGHT showed a trend toward more accepting attitudes on four of the six categories.

Self-reported drug use data were gathered on 11 drugs: alcohol, caffeine, nicotine, marijuana, cocaine, narcotics, amphetamines, tranquilizers, barbiturates, hallucinogens, and inhalants. For most of the drugs usage was minimal. Caffeine and tobacco were the only exceptions with the highest median use for all groups.

The drugs were grouped into subsets of legal, legal/prescription, and illegal for analysis.

Table 3 shows the results of the Wilcoxon test on the aggregated substance use data. No significant changes were found in the drug usage patterns of any of the groups from the pretest to the posttest. Usage levels appeared to remain the same throughout the subjects' participation in the substance abuse course. A comparison of the usage levels between groups revealed that SPAN did show more use than the NSPAN group but no significant difference in use between SPAN and NIGHT. On the pretest, SPAN's higher usage was in the area of both legal and illegal drugs. However, on the posttest, the only notable difference is in the area of legal drugs. SPAN reported using more tobacco and caffeine, but less alcohol than NSPAN on the pretest; SPAN also reported more cocaine and marijuana use on the pretest. On the posttest, SPAN continued to show higher use of tobacco and caffeine, but no difference in alcohol, cocaine and marijuana. The drug usage patterns of SPAN and NIGHT were similar except for the posttest use of legal drugs. NIGHT reduced their consumption of caffeine and alcohol and increased marijuana and cocaine use. However, none of the small increases and decreases were substantial enough to be called significant at the .05 level.

Kendall Tau Correlation Coefficients were calculated on the attitude and drug use data subsets of legal, legal prescription and illegal drugs for both the pretest and the posttest for each group; however, no consistent relationships emerged.

DISCUSSION OF FINDINGS

Caution must be exercised in assuming that the findings of this study would be applicable to all former abusers/offenders. Since the participants completed a rigorous selection process, they may represent a segment of abusers/offenders who are motivated to take full advantage of the support and opportunities of aftercare.

Table 3

Combined Median Scores for Substance Use Subsets for All Groups on Pretest and Posttest

Subset	SPAN		NSPAN		NIGHT		OVERALL	
	Pretest	Posttest	Pretest	Posttest	Pretest	Posttest	Pre	Post
Legal	2.4	2.7*	2.1	1.9[a]	2.1	1.9[a]	2.2	2.2
Legal/Prescription	1.1	1.1	1.0	1.0	1.1	1.1	1.0	1.0
Illegal	1.5	1.1[b]	1.1	1.0[b]	1.3	1.4**	1.3	1.1

*Subset showed a non-significant increase in drug usage (caffeine).

**Subset showed a non-significant increase in drug usage (cocaine, marijuana).

[a]Subset showed a non-significant decrease in drug use (caffeine, alcohol).

[b]Subset showed a non-significant decrease in drug use (cocaine, marijuana).

Knowledge

The finding that all three groups increased their knowledge levels was not surprising given previous research which has shown that gains in drug and alcohol knowledge are associated with most educational programs (Blum et al., 1976; Schmidt et al., 1977; Swisher, 1974). It was encouraging to find that the increase in knowledge was not accompanied by increases in drug use as a few other studies have demonstrated (Ray, 1978; Schaps et al., 1978). The finding of less drug and alcohol knowledge on the part of the SPAN group of former abusers did not support other research which concluded that users are more knowledgeable than non-users (Fejer & Smart, 1973). However, the SPAN group's lower knowledge level does support the suggestion by Marlatt and Gordon (1980) and Marlatt and Marques (1977) that former abusers are in need of education as to the physical and psychological effects of drugs and alcohol. SPAN's ability to increase their knowledge and to narrow the gap between themselves and one of the groups of regular college students could be viewed as beneficial if several assumptions are made. If it is assumed that increased knowledge is desirable in and of itself and if it is assumed that the increase in knowledge is somehow related to the group's participation in the university course, then it would appear that the inclusion of such a course in the aftercare program was beneficial to the SPAN group. If it is assumed that an increase in drug and alcohol knowledge helps to counteract the previously demonstrated attribution of magical effects to the drugs themselves (McGuire et al., 1966; Tamerin et al., 1970) and thus plays a part in the prevention of relapse, then providing an opportunity to former abusers to increase their knowledge can be viewed as beneficial. If it is assumed that knowledge serves in some way as a basis for decision making and for attitude formation, then it would be important to rectify knowledge deficiencies and inaccuracies.

Without the existence of a control group in this study, it cannot be concluded that the university course per se caused the increased knowledge in any of the three groups. Alternative explanations include an increased ability to take the examination possibly as a result of the pretest, an increase as an artifact of the baseline, reading the text, and/or experiences external to the course.

The inclusion of the SPAN group of former abusers in a classroom did not appear to adversely affect the cognitive processes of the regular college students. The NSPAN group increased their knowledge levels significantly and even surpassed the NIGHT group who were not exposed to the former abusers. Alternate explanations for the achievement of the NSPAN group would include the fact that they were younger than NIGHT, and attending school full time for the most part, and thus may have been able to devote more time to studying and may have been more familiar with and possibly less anxious about taking tests. NIGHT group members were employed full time and this could have contributed to their lesser achievement in the course.

Attitudes

Previous research had shown that knowledge alone had no discernible effect on attitudes (Goodstadt, 1974; Swisher, 1974; Swisher & Warner, 1974). However, some studies in which cognitive and affective approaches were included in the education have shown attitude changes in a desirable direction (Blum et al., 1976; Carney, 1974; Swisher & Horan, 1974; Swisher & Horman, 1974; Swisher & Piniuk, 1974). Additionally, one study showed that the use of ex-addicts produced attitudes less favorable to drug use (Richards, 1970). The SPAN group of former abusers and their classmates showed significant attitude change in some areas, on normative issues for both and on regulatory issues and legal drugs for NSPAN. These changes were in a desirable direction toward the less accepting end of the scale. The NIGHT group, on the other hand, showed a trend toward more accepting attitudes and significantly so in the area of illegal drugs. The findings that the NIGHT group changed their attitudes in the opposite direction from SPAN and NSPAN could indicate that the presence of the former abusers in the classroom contributed to an attitude change toward the less accepting end of the scale. An alternative explanation of the NIGHT group's attitude change could have resulted from their greater life experience because of their age, or the amount of stress they were under from working full time and attending school part time, or perhaps some other dynamic which was operating in their classrooms, for example, interaction with students currently using drugs and/or alcohol.

The finding that the NSPAN group exposed to the SPAN group of former abusers did not become more accepting in their attitudes should be encouraging to the university and alleviate concerns over adverse effects of integrating the former abusers into the classroom with regular college students.

SPAN had significantly higher use levels on the pretest than did their classmates (NSPAN), but this did not correlate with an increase in their classmates' level and, in fact, non-significant reductions in use occurred. This finding should be reassuring to the sponsoring university, and is also supportive of a few studies that have shown education to be preventive of drug use (Carney, 1974; Slimmon, 1973; Swisher & Piniuk, 1974).

Correlations between Attitudes and Use

The correlation coefficients did not consistently support any relationships between attitudes and use. Other research has found concurrence between attitudes and use, especially when the attitude is based on actual behavior (Banks et al., 1981; Zanna et al., 1980). In the present study the results of the correlation between attitudes and behavior were mixed.

The former abusers could not be distinguished by their attitudes from other groups of regular college students. This possibly supports previous research on the attitudes of ex-smokers and nonsmokers who were shown to have more similar attitudes than exsmokers and current smokers (Baer, 1966; Rosenblatt, 1967; Sorochan, 1969).

Drug Use

SPAN showed a non-significant decrease in their drug usage except for caffeine. Their higher use of tobacco and caffeine than the other groups is not an unusual phenomenon (Ray, 1978). This seems to be indicative that with the so-called triple addiction of alcohol, caffeine and tobacco, the reduction or elimination of alcohol does not necessarily result in the reduction or elimination of physical dependence on the other drugs and may in fact increase it.

CONCLUSIONS

The conclusions from the study are as follows:

1. Substance abuse education for former abusers/offenders warrants consideration as part of an aftercare program. The former abusers' lower levels of knowledge can be increased. While enrolled in the substance abuse course, the former abusers increased

their knowledge, reinforced attitudes which were less accepting of society's use of drugs and alcohol, and maintained minimal levels of substance use.

2. Substance abuse education for former abusers/offenders should continue to be sponsored by the university, as no discernible detrimental effects occurred to the regular college students exposed to the SPAN group. The regular college students so exposed increased their knowledge significantly, maintained less accepting attitudes and minimal drug usage throughout the course. There is some evidence to suggest that the inclusion of the former abusers in the classroom mitigated the occurrence of some possibly undesirable effects, since the regular college students who were not exposed exhibited attitudes which were generally more accepting of drug and alcohol use by society and some non-significant increases in drug use.

3. The selection process utilized to recruit the SPAN students appears to be sufficiently rigorous to reduce the possibility of academic failure and/or problem students.

REFERENCES

Adams, S., & McArthur, V. *Performance of narcotic-involved prison releasees under three kinds of community experience* (Research Report No. 16). Washington, D.C.: Department of Corrections, June 1969.

Baer, D. J. Smoking attitude, behavior and beliefs of college males. *Journal of Social Psychology*, 1966, *68*, 65-78.

Banks, M. H., Bewley, B. R., & Blanc, J. M. Adolescent attitudes to smoking: Their influence on behavior. *International Journal of Health Education*, 1981, *24*(1), 39-44.

Beckett, G. E., & Thomas, E. Understanding honored: Court dispositions of early, drug free discharges from California Civil Addict Program. *Journal of Drug Issues*, 1976, *6*(2), 191-195.

Berecochea, J., & Sing, G. E. The effectiveness of a halfway house for civilly committed narcotics addicts. *International Journal of the Addictions*, 1972, *7*(1), 123-132.

Blum, R. H., Blum, E., & Garfield, E. *Drug education: Results and recommendations.* Lexington, Mass.: D. C. Heath, 1976.

Brown, J. S. (Ed.). *Addicts and aftercare: Community integration of the former drug user.* (Vol. 3). Beverly Hills, Calif.: Sage Publications, 1979.

Carney, R. E. Valuing and drugs: Final, 1970-71, report on the Tempe, Arizona, drug abuse prevention program. In *Why evaluate drug education? Report of a task force, May, 1974, enhancing drug education in the south.* Atlanta, Ga.: Southern Regional Education Board, 1974.

Chaney, E. R., O'Leary, M. R., & Marlatt, G. A. Skill training with alcoholics. *Journal of Consulting and Clinical Psychology*, 1978, *46*(5), 1092-1104.

Dole, V. P., & Nyswander, M. E. Methadone maintenance treatment, a ten-year perspective. *Journal of the American Medical Association*, 1976, *235*, 2117-2119.

Dole, V. P., Nyswander, M. E., & Warner, A. Successful treatment of 750 criminal addicts. *Journal of the American Medical Association*, 1968, *206*, 2708-2714.

Elliot, D. S., & Ross, H. L. *Delinquency and dropout.* Lexington, Mass.: Lexington Books, 1974.

Fairweather, G. The development, evaluation and diffusion of rehabilitative programs: A social change process. In L. I. Stein & M. A. Test (Eds.), *Alternatives to mental hospital treatment.* New York: Plenum, 1978.

Falanga, R. E. Pyramid Project, Pacific Institute for Research and Evaluation, Lafayette, Calif. Personal communication, January 1980.

Fejer, D., & Smart, R. G. The knowledge about drugs, attitudes towards them and the drug use rates of high school students. *Journal of Drug Education,* 1973, *3,* 377-388.

Frease, D. E. The schools, self-concept and juvenile delinquency. *British Journal of Criminology,* 1972, *12,* 133-146.

Goodstadt, M. (Ed.). *Research on methods and programs of drug education.* Ontario, Canada: Addiction Research Foundation, 1974.

Griffin, R. N., & James E. *Evaluation of the Human Services Paraprofessional Certificate Program.* Unpublished report for the School of Social Welfare, San Diego State University, October 1979.

Hawkins, J. D. Reintegrating street drug abusers—community roles in continuing care. In B. S. Brown (Ed.), *Addicts and aftercare: Community integration of the former drug user* (Vol. 3). Beverly Hills, Calif.: Sage Publications, 1979.

Hawkins, J. D. Personal communication, January 1980.

Hirschi, T. *Causes of delinquency.* Berkeley: University of California Press, 1969.

Hogges, R., & Hogges, L. *An exploratory study in transition.* U.S. Educational Resources Information Center, 1976. (ERIC Document Reproduction Service No. ED 127 540)

Kaplan, H. B., & Meyerowitz, J. Evaluation of a half-way house: Integrated community approach in the rehabilitation of narcotic addicts. *International Journal of the Addictions,* 1969, *4*(1), 65-76.

Katz, H. A. California Rehabilitation Center: A critical look. *International Journal of the Addictions,* 1977, *6*(3), 543-551.

Kelly, D. H., & Balch, R. W. Social origins and school failure. *Pacific Sociological Review,* 1971, *14,* 413-430.

Kramer, J. C., & Bass, R. A. Institutionalization patterns among civilly committed addicts. *Journal of the American Medical Association,* 1969, *208*(12), 2297-2301.

Kramer, J. C., Bass, R. A., & Berecochea, J. E. Civil commitment for addicts. The California program. *American Journal of Psychiatry,* 1968, *125*(5), 816-824.

Lynn, R., & Nash, G. A study of seven prison based drug abuse treatment programs. *Drug Abuse Treatment Information Project.* Montclair State College, Montclair, New Jersey, October 1975.

Mann, M. Attitude: Key to successful treatment. In G. E. Staub (Ed.), *The paraprofessional in the treatment of alcoholism.* Springfield, Ill.: Charles C Thomas, 1973.

Marlatt, G. A. Craving for alcohol, loss of control and relapse: A cognitive-behavioral analysis. In P. E. Nathan, G. A. Marlatt, & T. Loberg (Eds.), *Alcoholism: New dimensions in behavioral research and treatment.* New York: Plenum, 1978.

Marlatt, G. A. Personal communication, January 1980.

Marlatt, G. A., & Gordon, J. R. Determinants of relapse: Implications for the maintenance of behavior change. In P. Davidson (Ed.), *Behavioral medicine: Changing health lifestyles.* New York: Brunner/Mazel, 1980.

Marlatt, G. A., & Marques, J. K. Meditation, self-control and alcohol use. In R. B. Stuart (Ed.), *Behavioral self-management: Strategies, techniques and outcomes.* New York: Brunner/Mazel, 1977.

McGuire, M. T., Mendelson, J. H., & Stein, S. Comparative psychosocial studies of alcoholic and non-alcoholic subjects undergoing experimentally-induced ethanol intoxication. *Psychosomatic Medicine,* 1966, *28,* 13-25.

McKee, J. M. *New directions in corrections.* U.S. Educational Resources Information Center, 1971. (ERIC Document Reproduction Service No. ED 059 445)

McVey, R. F. *Establishing a college orientation program for ex-offenders.* U.S. Educational Resources Information Center, 1977. (ERIC Document Reproduction Service No. ED 147 677)

Pittel, S. M. Addict aftercare: Essence or afterthought. *Contemporary Drug Problems*, 1977, *6*, 491-513. (a)

Pittel, S. M. *Community support systems for addict aftercare*. Walnut Creek, Calif.: Pacific Institute for Research and Evaluation, 1977. (b)

Platt, J. J., & Labate, C. Recidivism in youthful heroin offenders and characteristics of parole behavior and environment. *International Journal of the Addictions*, 1976, *11*(4), 651-657.

Prager, A., & Goldberg, J. *National program for selected population segments*. Project summaries. U.S. Educational Resources Information Center, 1977. (ERIC Document Reproduction Service No. ED 146 376)

Ray, O. S. *Drugs, society and human behavior*. St. Louis: C. V. Mosby, 1978.

Richards, L. G. Psychological sophistication in current drug abuse education. In J. R. Wittenborn, J. P. Smith, & S. A. Wittenborn (Eds.), *Communications and drug abuse*. Springfield, Ill.: Charles C Thomas, 1970.

Rosenblatt, D., Rosen, B., & Allen, H. Attitudes, information and behavior of college students related to smoking and smoking cessation. In S. V. Zagona (Ed.), *Studies and issues in smoking behavior*. Tuscon: University of Arizona Press, 1967.

Sakumoto, K. N. *Attachment to delinquent friends: Peer influences and delinquent involvement*. Unpublished master's thesis, University of Washington, 1978.

Schaps, E., DiBartolo, R., Paley, C. S., & Churgin, S. *Primary prevention evaluation research: A review of 127 program evaluations*. Walnut Creek, Calif.: Pacific Institute for Research and Evaluation, 1978.

Schmidt, W. K., Burchiel, S. W., & Meyers, F. H. The pharmacology of drug abuse—a novel approach to drug education at San Quentin. *Drug and Alcohol Dependence*, 1977, *2*, 175-183.

Simon, S., Kirschenbaum, H., & Howe, L. *Values clarification*. New York: Hart Publishing Co., 1978.

Slimmon, L. *Alternatives and values clarification*. Annual Report, County of Marin, July 10, 1973.

Smart, R. G. Outcome studies of therapeutic community and halfway house treatment for addicts. *International Journal of the Addictions*, 1976, *11*(1), 153-159.

Sorochan, W. D. *Attitudes of secondary school health educators of Kentucky toward smoking and health*. Unpublished doctoral dissertation, School of Health, Physical Education and Recreation, Indiana University, August 1969.

Special Program in Alcohol and Narcotics (SPAN). 1196 Broadway, San Diego, CA 92101 (619) 233-5285.

Stanton, D. M. The client as family member: Aspects of continuing treatment. In B. S. Brown (Ed), *Addicts and aftercare: Community integration of the former drug user* (Vol. 3). Beverly Hills, Calif.: Sage Publications, 1979.

Sultan, P., & Ehmann, G. E. *The employment of persons with arrest records and the ex-offender*. U.S. Educational Resources Information Center, 1970. (ERIC Document Reproduction Service No. ED 047 241)

Swisher, J. D. The effectiveness of drug education: Conclusions based on experimental evaluations. In M. Goodstadt (Ed.), *Research on methods and programs of drug education*. Ontario, Canada: Addiction Research Foundation, 1974.

Swisher, J. D., & Horan, J. J. Effecting drug attitude change in college students via induced cognitive dissonance. In M. Goodstadt (Ed.), *Myths and methodology in drug education: A critical review of the research evidence*. Substudy No. 588. Toronto, Canada: Addiction Research Foundation, 1974.

Swisher, J. D., & Horman, R. E. Drug abuse prevention. In M. Goodstadt (Ed.), *Myths and methodology in drug education: A critical review of the research evidence*. Substudy No. 588. Toronto, Canada: Addiction Research Foundation, 1974.

Swisher, J. D., & Piniuk, A. J. An evaluation of Keystone Central School District's drug education program. In M. Goodstadt (Ed.), *Myths and methodology in drug education: A critical review of the research evidence.* Substudy No. 588. Toronto, Canada: Addiction Research Foundation, 1974.

Swisher, J. D., & Warner, R. W. *A study of four approaches to drug abuse education.* Final Report to the U.S. Department of Health, Education, and Welfare, Office of Education, Bureau of Research, 1974.

Tamerin, J. S., Weiner, S., & Mendelson, J. H. Alcoholics' expectancies of recall of experiences during intoxication. *American Journal of Psychiatry,* 1970, *126,* 1697-1704.

Test, M. A., & Stein, L. I. Training in community living: Research design and results. In L. I. Stein & M. A. Test (Eds.), *Alternatives to mental hospital treatment.* New York: Plenum, 1978.

Wepner, S. F. Which way drug education? *Journal of Drug Education,* 1979, *9*(2), 93-103.

Wittenborn, J. R., Smith, J. P., & Wittenborn, S. A. (Eds.). *Communications and drug abuse.* Springfield, Ill.: Charles C Thomas, 1970.

Wurmser, L. *The hidden dimension: Psychodynamics in compulsive drug use.* New York: Jason Aronson, 1978.

Zanna, M., Olson, J., & Fazio, R. Attitude-behavior consistency: An individual perspective. *Journal of Personality and Social Psychology,* 1980, *38*(3), 431-440.

The Effects of a Self-Esteem Counseling Group on Male Prisoners' Self-Concept

Judith R. Vicary
Roland Good

ABSTRACT. A self-esteem counseling workshop was conducted for fifteen male inmates of a therapeutic community within a minimum-medium security state prison. Participant offenses included drugs, burglary, aggressive offenses and murder; most were 19-25 years old, serving 2½-5-year sentences. The program emphasized family related self-concept, using experiential and discussion strategies. Topics covered included family antecedents of self-perception, self-assessment and acceptance, behavioral demonstration of self worth, and current family interactions and effects. Results indicated a significant increase in the participants' family-based self-esteem scores from pre- to posttest, while no change occurred in peer or work-oriented self-concept.

When the prison gates slam behind an inmate, he does not lose his human quality, his mind does not become closed to ideas, his intellect does not cease to feed on a free and open interchange of opinions; his yearning for self-esteem does not end; nor his quest for self realization conclude. If anything the needs for identity and self-esteem are more compelling.

Justice Thurgood Marshall

Judith R. Vicary, PhD, is a Postdoctoral Research Fellow, National Institute of Drug Abuse, Department of Individual and Family Studies, The Pennsylvania State University, University Park, PA 16802. Roland Good, MS, is a doctoral candidate, Program in School Psychology, The Pennsylvania State University, University Park, PA 16802.

Background

These words are particularly important for prison rehabilitation and counseling program considerations. While the question of low self-concept as a predictor or cause of criminal behavior has not been resolved, it has been acknowledged that many offenders, both juvenile and adult, male and female, have low self-concept scores (Lively, Dinitz, & Reckless, 1962; Kay, 1962; Clarke & Hasler, 1967; Light, 1976; Lund & Salary, 1980). Seiber (1980) notes that "inmates enter prison with little self-esteem or individual pride, and what they might retain from the street is stripped away by the regimentation and daily psychological degradations. . . They are faced with a completely negative system. . ." (p. 27). This negativism is seen even more clearly in many "therapeutic community" approaches used within various prisons. These are deliberately designed to break down an inmate's defenses, using confrontation, total honesty, and self and others' criticism. While these intense measures have value in the stripping away of excuses, blame and justification, they also leave a participant with an even lower self-appraisal, and rarely, if ever, is this problem addressed.

Self-concept has several components or sources, and can be measured relative to relationships or situations, e.g., peer/friend-related self-concept, work or school influenced, and family-associated self-perceptions. The dimension pertaining to family has particular importance for successful parole, and low rearrest rates. Ohlin (1954) determined that 75 percent of inmates with close family ties while in prison did better in fulfilling parole requirements. In two studies Glaser's (1969) findings were similar, and Schneller (1976) reports that California Department of Corrections results showed that for inmates with continued contact with families during incarceration, seventy percent were "arrest free" during their first year on parole. Holt and Miller (1972) also found a much lower recidivism rate for prisoners who had regular family visits during incarceration, and other parole success indicators were not as effective predictors as that of having a family to go home to. They concluded that parolees living with either parents or wives were somewhat less likely to violate their parole. Encouraging strong family ties is obviously an important consideration in promoting correctional effectiveness. One major way to facilitate this goal is to improve a prisoner's sense of worth in relation to his family. Therefore, this study was designed to examine the effectiveness of a self-concept workshop in improving self-esteem, and to explore possible factors which may affect the effectiveness of the workshop.

The study examined five areas of self-esteem: locus of control, family-related self-concept, peer-related self-concept, school/work related self-concept, and self-confidence. The areas are referred to as control, family, peer, work, and self, respectively, in the following discussion.

Program Subjects

In an effort to improve the self-esteem of prisoners in an eastern minimum-medium security state prison, a self-esteem counseling workshop was developed under the auspices of the Director of Treatment, and led by a rehabilitation counselor from outside the prison staff. The inmate participants were volunteer residents of a therapeutic community within the prison, representative of the general population, considered "rough" men, not the best or "elite" prisoners. Their crimes included drug offenses, burglary, aggressive offenses, and murder. The majority of the men were in the 19-25 age range, 50% each black and white, and serving average sentences of two- and one-half- to five years.

The therapeutic community is run primarily by the prisoners, with a hierarchy of responsibilities and leadership positions based on inmate-developed rules. Once a week for approximately one- and one-half hours the men voluntarily participate in their choice of workshops offered by community professionals, e.g., public speaking, values clarification. Participants do not receive any system benefits for joining the group, that is, parole considerations, privileges, etc. The subjects in this study had spent three months or less in the therapeutic community and had not yet achieved high levels of responsibility. Many had aggressive problems and were described by the treatment staff as "severely damaged human beings." Twenty men signed up to participate in one of two self-esteem workshops offered, each lasting ten weeks. The first workshop group had six participants who completed the program; the second session had nine participants. The other five men began each program but were unable to finish because of status changes, e.g., transfer, new trial, parole. The age of the prisoners was coded as either young (below 25, $n = 8$), or old (over 25, $n = 7$). Education was coded as either high school graduate or equivalent ($n = 11$), or less than high school level ($n = 4$). Marital status was coded as either single, not living with someone (n = 8), or married or living with someone (n = 7). The number of previously held jobs was coded as one job or less (n = 4), or more than one job (n = 11). Six of the prisoners were black, and nine were white.

Program Content

The program focused on family-related self-esteem, believed to be both extremely important to the inmates as a support group, and that aspect possibly amenable to change while in the prison environment. For example, school or work-associated self worth could not be behaviorally addressed because the men were not in school or work activities. The course sequence was developed from the work of Elkins (1977) and assorted values exercises (Howe & Howe, 1975), plus original materials by Vicary. Topics included the early antecedents of self-concept, particularly as they related to family; childhood perceptions of self; behaviors and activities reflecting how one feels about himself; self assessment of present strengths and areas wished to be improved; self-acceptance; current family importance and feedback; consequences of one's self-concept; how one affects the self-image of others, particularly family members; and activities to begin and continue with family to enhance each other's self-esteem. The activities and discussions were shared by the inmates with their families through phone calls, letters and furlough visits home. The extent of their sharing the workshop experience far exceeded the leader's planned or hoped-for level and was an "unobtrusive measure" of their growing involvement in and commitment to the sessions. While the groups began as "leader-led," the participants took increasing responsibility for initiating, sharing, encouraging one another, giving and seeking feedback, and self-disclosure.

Research Questions

Part I:

1. Was there any change in overall prisoner self-esteem as a result of participation in a workshop?
2. Were any areas of self-esteem higher or lower than other areas of self-esteem?

3. Did the amount of change in prisoner self-esteem depend upon the area of self-esteem examined?

Part II:

1. Was the level of prisoner self-esteem different as a function of the number of jobs the prisoner had held prior to incarceration (n jobs), the workshop group the prisoner attended (group), or the prisoner's age, race, education, or marital status (marital)?
2. Did age, race, education, marital, jobs, or group affect the outcome of the workshop?

Methods

The Educational Quality Assessment Self-Esteem scale (Hertzog & Seiverling, 1978; Miller, 1976) was used to measure the inmates' self-esteem, with the fifth grade reading level version selected to accommodate any academic limitations. The final scale consisted of 48 Likert type items, with 9 items on the control subscale, 8 items on the family subscale, 6 items on the work subscale, 13 items on the peer subscale, and 12 items on the self subscale. Two types of scores were used from the EQA Self-Esteem scale. In the analysis of Part I, the average item response was computed for each subscale so subscale scores would be comparable in spite of differing numbers of items on each scale. In the analysis of Part II, the total for each subscale was used.

All subjects were administered the self-esteem measure before and after participation in the workshop. The experimental design was thus a pretest, posttest no control design (Campbell & Stanley, 1963; Cook & Campbell, 1979) with the most important threats to the internal validity of this type of study being the effects of maturation and history. Maturation would be a factor if subjects entered the workshops with a low leel of self-esteem because they were beginning the tearing down process and left the workshop later as they were engaged in a building-up process in the therapeutic community. History would be a factor if there were a change in the prison environment that increased prisoner self-esteem during the workshop. These threats are controlled to some extent by examining self-esteem in areas other than the emphasis of the workshop. A change in the prisoners or the prison environment would be expected to affect all areas of self-esteem equally. A specific change in family-related self-concept would be evidence of a workshop effect.

Part I

In answering the questions in Part I, a two-way within-subjects analysis of variance was used, with time of measurement (time) and area of self-esteem (area) as the two factors. This design, described further in Myers (1979, p. 188), allows for tests of a main effect of time (question 1), a main effect of area (question 2), and the interaction between time and area (question 3).

Part II

In addressing the questions in Part II, gain scores were computed by subtracting the pretest score from posttest score for each self-concept area. The gain scores were then analyzed in a 7-way mixed effects analysis of variance. The general layout for mixed effects analysis of variance is presented in Myers (1979, pp. 199-227). Age, race, education, marital, jobs, and group were the between-subject factors, and area was the within-subjects factor. The main effects of the between-subjects factor were included in the design, and the two-way interactions between area and each of the between subjects factors were also assessed, but higher order interactions were not included. Any variability associated with the higher order interactions was thus confounded with the error terms. Higher order interactions were not examined because of the small sample size. It should be noted that an analysis of gain scores is computationally equivalent to examining group-time interactions (Levin & Marascuilo, 1977).

Because of unequal sample sizes in each cell of the design, this design is described as unbalanced with the resulting differences in computing and interpreting the sums of squares for each effect. The method of equally weighing the cell means was used in this analysis. This method provides a test of the effect of interest given all other effects in the model. This procedure is further described in Myers (1979, pp. 388-404).

The analysis conducted in Part II was considered exploratory in nature, designed to provide possible directions for further research and to explore a wide range of effects. As an exploratory analysis it has low power to detect significant effects and a high chance of type

I error, so findings from this section of the study should be interpreted with caution. The Bonferroni Additive Inequality was used to control the family-wise type I error in the resulting family of 25 contrasts (Myers, 1979, pp. 298-300).

RESULTS

Part I

The results of the two-way within subjects analysis of variance are reported in Table 1. These results indicate that there was a significant interaction between time and area. This interaction is portrayed graphically in Figure 1. A follow-up analysis was then conducted on the interaction effect. Differences between areas were evaluated for significance at each level of time, and differences between times were evaluated for significance at each level of area.

Results of the follow-up analysis are presented in Table 2. Means

TABLE 1

Time by Area Analysis of Variance

Summary Table

Source	df	SS	MS	F
Area	4	4.06	1.01	4.16**
Error	56	13.66	.24	
Test	1	1.20	1.20	5.48*
Error	14	3.07	.22	
Area* Test	4	.89	.22	3.80**
Error	56	3.28	.06	
Total	149	34.41		

*p < .05.

**p < .01.

FIGURE 1

Plot of Self-Esteem Means

By Time and Area

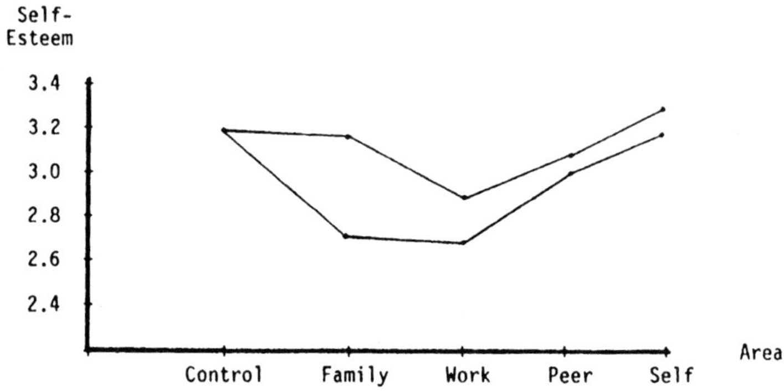

TABLE 2

Self-Esteem Means

By Area and Time

	Area				
Time	Control	Family	Work	Peer	Self
Pretest	A 3.19	BC 2.72*	B 2.69	AC 2.98	A 3.18
Posttest	A 3.19	A 3.18*	B 2.88	AB 3.12	A 3.29

at the same level of time which share a common letter are not significantly different, and means in the same area which are marked by an asterisk are significantly different. Thus, there was no significant difference between pre- and posttest scores in the control, work, peer, and self areas, but there was a significant gain in self-esteem in the family area.

Similarly, on the pretest there were no significant differences among the control, peer, and self areas, and they were all significantly higher than the work area. The family and work areas were not significantly different, and the family and peer areas were not significantly different. The family area was significantly lower than the control and self areas. On the posttest, the control, family, peer, and self areas were not significantly different, and the work area was significantly lower than all other areas except the peer area.

Part II

The results of the seven-way mixed effects analysis of variance are presented in Table 3. There were no significant effects or interactions in this analysis. Thus, there was no evidence to indicate

TABLE 3

Analysis of Variance Summary Table

Part II

Source	df	SS	MS	F
Group	1	5.98	5.98	0.15
Age	1	17.64	17.64	0.45
Education	1	55.66	55.66	1.43
Marital Status	1	12.42	12.42	0.32
Number of Jobs	1	90.70	90.70	2.33
Race	1	22.50	22.50	0.58
Error	8	311.74	38.97	
Area	4	64.64	16.16	1.80
Group*Area	4	54.23	13.56	1.51
Age*Area	4	27.96	6.99	0.78
Education*Area	4	53.95	13.49	1.50
Marital*Area	4	48.61	12.15	1.35
Njobs*Area	4	34.67	8.67	0.96
Race*Area	4	32.51	8.13	0.90
Error	32	287.63	8.99	
Total	74	1226.19		

Note: Sums of squares do not add to the total sums of squares because an equally weighted means analysis was used (Myers, 1979, pp. 388-404).

that either age, race, education, number of jobs, marital status, or group affected the self-esteem of the inmates or the effectiveness of the workshop as identified in part I.

Conclusions

There was a significant interaction between the time and area of self-esteem measured. This interaction indicates that the change in self-esteem from before to after the workshop varied with the area examined, and that differences between areas of self-esteem were different after the workshop than they were before. The interaction appeared to be due to a significant increase in self-esteem in the family-related area, with no significant change in any of the other areas. On the pretest, family and work were areas of lowest self-esteem compared to control and self, and peer was in between. On the posttest, family was with control and self as areas of high self-esteem relative to work, with peer again in between.

Thus, the workshop appeared to increase family-related self-concept. It is unlikely that this change was a result of history or maturation effects since history and maturation would be expected to affect all areas of self-esteem equally. There was no evidence in this study that race, age, education, marital status, number of jobs held, or workshop attended affected the gain in self-concept in the family-related area. However, this finding should be interpreted cautiously due to the low power to detect an effect if there was one. The importance of family relationships and support to successful parole following incarceration has been shown previously. In addition, it is obvious that prison generally does nothing to enhance an inmate's self-esteem yet it is a vitally important factor in rehabilitation success. Bennett (1979) notes that:

> nurturing of better self-concepts . . . (relates) to enhancing the status of the inmate as an individual, as a contributing member of society, and as a worthwhile person. In essence, the evidence points toward improvement of an individual's self-esteem as being a key to a more adequate post-institutional adjustment. (p. 3)

The fact that family-related self-concept appears to be amenable to improvement in the prison setting should have implications for rehabilitation goals and subsequent programming planning.

REFERENCES

Bennett, L. Connections adrift—enhancing self-control could help. *Headway*. Minneapolis, Minnesota: Minneapolis Medical Research Foundation, 1979.

Campbell, D. T., & Stanley, J. C. *Experimental and quasi-experimental designs for research.* Chicago: Rand McNally, 1963.

Clarke, W., & Hasler, K. Differentiation of criminals and non-criminals with a self-concept measure. *Psychological Reports,* 1967, *20,* 623-632.

Cook, T. D., & Campbell, D. T. *Quasi-experimentation: Design and analysis issues for field settings.* Chicago: Rand McNally, 1979.

Elkins, D. *Teaching people to love themselves.* Rochester, New York: Growth Associates, 1977.

Glaser, D. *The effectiveness of prison and parole system.* New York: Bobbs-Merrill Co., 1969.

Hertzog, J. F., & Seiverling, R. F. *Educational Quality Assessment: Manual for interpreting intermediate school reports.* Harrisburg: Pennsylvania Department of Education, 1978.

Holt, N., & Miller, D. Explorations in inmate-family relationships. Research Report No. 46, California Department of Corrections, Sacramento, California, 1972.

Howe, L., & Howe, M. *Personalizing education: Values clarification and beyond.* New York: Hart Publishing Co., 1975.

Kay, B. Female prisoners: Their concepts of self. *Police,* 1962, *7*(2), 39-41.

Levin, J. R., & Marascuilo, L. A. Post hoc analysis of repeated measures interactions and gain scores: Whither the inconsistency? *Psychological Bulletin,* 1977, *84,* 247-248.

Light, H. *Highly competent girls and delinquent girls: A comparative study of value needs and self-concept profiles.* Unpublished doctoral dissertation, Michigan State University, 1976.

Lively, E., Dinitz, S., & Reckless, W. Self-concept as a predictor of juvenile delinquency. *American Journal of Orthopsychology,* 1962, *32,* 159-169.

Lund, N., & Salary, H. Measured self-concept in adjudicated juvenile offenders. *Adolescence,* 1980, Vol. XV. No. 57, 65-73.

Miller, K. R. *A guide to the analysis and interpretation of EQA scores and related intervention techniques: Goal I self-esteem.* Harrisburg: Pennsylvania Department of Education, 1976.

Myers, J. L. *Fundamentals of Experimental Design* (3rd Ed.). Boston: Allyn & Bacon, 1979.

Ohlin, L. *The stability and validity of parole experience tables.* Unpublished doctoral dissertation, University of Chicago, 1954.

Seiber, L. A course in self-esteem. *American Education,* 1980, 24-27.